CONTAINER
GARDENS
BY NUMBER

CONTAINER GARDENS BY NUMBER

50 Colorful Plant-by-Number Plans for Hanging Baskets, Pots, and Window Boxes

Bob Purnell

Reader's Digest

The Reader's Digest Association, Inc.
Pleasantville, New York/Montreal

Thanks to my mom, Carol, for her unfailing support, and to Judy Holbrook and Andy Luft for their invaluable input and friendship.

A READER'S DIGEST BOOK

This edition published by The Reader's Digest Association by arrangement with Hamlyn, a division of Octopus Publishing Group Ltd., 2–4 Heron Quays, London E14 4JP

U.S. Project Editor: Miranda Smith
Project Designer: George McKeon
Executive Editor, Trade Publishing: Dolores York
Associate Publisher, Trade Publishing: Christopher T. Reggio
Vice President and Publisher, Trade Publishing: Harold Clarke

Library of Congress Cataloging-in-Publication Data

Purnell, Bob.
    Container gardens by number : 50 colorful plant-by-number plans for hanging baskets,
pots, and window boxes / Bob Purnell.
        p. cm.
    ISBN 0-7621-0497-X
    1.   Container gardening. I. Title.

SB418.P87 2004
635.9'86--dc22

2003061317

A NOTE TO OUR READERS

The 50 designs in *Container Gardens by Number* call for a total of more than 550 different plants. No garden center carries every species, much less every cultivar, included here, so in some instances you may have to make some substitutions. Carry this book with you and let a knowledgeable salesperson help select plants with both a similar appearance and cultural requirements to those in the book. When buying perennials, check to see whether they are hardy in your climate. If not, you'll need to overwinter those you want to save. Set the pots in a bright, airy spot that is cool but not freezing. Keep their soil slightly moist while the days are short and gray, and resume normal watering and fertilizing when they resume quick growth in the spring.

Address any comments about *Container Gardens by Number* to:
        The Reader's Digest Association, Inc.
        Adult Trade Publishing
        Reader's Digest Road
        Pleasantville, NY 10570-7000

For more Reader's Digest products and information, visit our website.

Printed in China

1 3 5 7 9 10 8 6 4 2

Contents

Introduction

Container gardening offers great flexibility. Not only can you grow just about any plant in a pot, but you can also move containers around to create a succession of new and eye-catching plant combinations. By using containers, you can produce a garden almost anywhere and, when necessary, move it to a new spot. You can transform a barren plot into a verdant oasis and bring it to life with splashes of vivid color. No garden is too small for at least one planted pot, window box or hanging basket. And best of all, you can achieve any effect almost instantly.

Left: Red dianthus, blue scaevola and yellow daisies create a riot of summer color in this hanging basket.

Because the range of plants suitable for container gardening is so wide, this book is designed to help you choose plants and containers that will be suitable not only for your garden and the growing conditions it offers but also for your lifestyle. A tranquil grouping of green foliage plants or a meditative Japanese area, for example, makes the perfect atmosphere to unwind at the end of a long, stressful workday. Or, a collection of succulents and other drought-tolerant plants may be appropriate if you are often away from home for several days at a time.

The planting schemes included in this book highlight groups of plants that look lovely together and that also flourish in the same basic growing conditions. Whether you have a large rambling garden, a tiny patio or just a windowsill, you are sure to find at least one container design in this book that is perfect for your personal situation.

How to use this book

The first section explains the basic principles of growing plants in containers and covers choosing pots and plants, grouping containers for maximum impact, and planting and general care, including troubleshooting. A good understanding of these principles will ensure success when re-creating the planting ideas detailed later in this book.

The remaining sections – covering pots, troughs, window boxes and hanging baskets – consist of a series of double-page spreads, each dedicated to a different container planting and tailored to a specific site or following a particular theme. Each scheme is realistic and uses plants that are widely available. You can copy designs exactly or, by using the information in the description, adapt them to fit your own circumstances and requirements. Each spread includes a full-color illustration of the container or group of containers, along with a description of the plants used, an explanation of why they have been chosen and details of any particular growing conditions they require. In addition, an overhead plan with a numbered key shows you exactly where to position each plant for the best effect. Side panels focus on groups of recommended plants, exploring their range and specific requirements. Of course, not every garden center will carry every species, much less every cultivar included here, so in some instances you may have to make some substitutions.

For a number of the plantings, an alternative scheme shows on the following spread. The alternative designs evoke an entirely different mood or work well on a site with radically different conditions.

Left: A row of simple galvanized buckets, planted with handsome variegated agaves and mulched with slate chips, achieves a crisp, classy effect.

Selecting containers

Containers come in all shapes, sizes and styles, from ornate and formal to understated and informal. Some containers can be used as focal features on their own, without any plants, while others simply hold a lush planting scheme. Whatever container you choose, make sure it suits the plants that are to grow in it and that both pot and plants suit their setting. Here we highlight some of the most available container types and explain their relative advantages and disadvantages.

Above: Terracotta pots are the most popular containers because their warm hues complement so many plants.

Terracotta

Perhaps the most common material used for ornamental pots, terracotta looks right in almost any setting. Hundreds of styles and shapes are available, from tall slender cylinders to low squat troughs. Because terracotta is porous it tends to dry out quickly, but this can be alleviated by lining the sides with polyethylene sheeting. In addition, always check that the pots you buy are guaranteed frost resistant: cheap terracotta seldom lasts beyond its first winter outdoors.

Plastic and fiberglass

Pots made from plastic are generally the cheapest option. However, there are some extremely convincing fiberglass pots that imitate stone, terracotta and lead that can be as expensive as the real thing. On the plus side, pots made from these materials are very light so they are easy to move around. They also dry out less quickly than porous containers and are resistant to frost, long-lasting and easy to clean. Avoid very cheap plastic containers unless you are looking for a short-term solution, because they usually discolor rapidly and can split within a year or two.

Stone and concrete

Reconstituted stone and concrete planters should last a lifetime and are often highly ornamental. They are ideal for long-term plantings and are generally frost resistant. The best examples can be quite expensive but are a worthwhile investment. The main disadvantage of these containers is their weight: this makes them extremely difficult to move, especially when planted, but also makes them more vandal- and theft-proof than other pots.

Glazed earthenware

Generally frost resistant, glazed pots often carry attractive patterns and come in a wide range of colors that can be used to enhance the plants grown in them. Considering their long life expectancy, they are relatively inexpensive and are often available with matching drip saucers. Sealing the base of these pots with silica sealant (silicone) allows them to be used for potted water features.

Timber

Pots and troughs made from timber have a natural appeal and can be custom built to fit a particular space. Paint or stain them to improve their appearance and line with polyethylene sheeting to prolong their lives. Half-barrels will last for years untreated, but flimsier troughs and window boxes require regular painting or varnishing in order to last well.

Metal

Planters made from lead have been in use for centuries, while galvanised and stainless steel or aluminium planters are more recent introductions. Metal containers suit contemporary gardens and complement a wide range of plants from grasses to vegetables. More than other types of containers, they can subject plant roots to extremes of temperature, so it is a good idea to line the inside with polyethylene sheeting before planting.

Hanging baskets

There are two basic types of hanging basket. The first is made from plastic or wire mesh and because of its open sides will need to be lined (see page 15). A second type is a hanging pot that can only be planted in the top. Open-sided mesh baskets create a fuller display because they can be planted all over, while hanging pots are easier to maintain.

Recycled

Almost any hollow object can be used as a container for growing plants, provided it will not disintegrate too quickly and you can make holes in the base for drainage. Old kettles, tin buckets, pipes, hollowed-out logs and even old sinks and lavatories make highly individual – and often amusing – homes for plants. You can frequently pick them up for next to nothing, so these are the cheapest containers of all.

Right: Metal containers lend a contemporary feeling and their reflective qualities make the most of a space.

Below right: Spiky phormiums and soft fuchsias merge successfully in this unusual hanging pot.

Below: Containers do not have to be crammed full of flowers and foliage. The beauty of this Grecian-style urn is accentuated by the plants in and around it.

Choosing plants

If you are determined enough, you can persuade just about any plant to grow in some kind of container, but some are better suited to the job than others. Certain plants positively thrive in pots and window boxes and often perform better than when planted in the open ground.

When deciding on plants for your containers, there are a few important factors to take into consideration.

Season of interest

First, and most importantly, most plants destined for growing in containers need to have a long season of interest.

Perennials such as delphiniums and lupins will grow perfectly well, but their flowering period is fairly short and they will spend the rest of the year looking unremarkable. However, perennials that flower over a long period, such as penstemons, chocolate cosmos (*Cosmos atrosanguineus*) and dainty white-flowered *Gaura lindheimeri*, are worth considering. Perennials that possess attractive foliage, such as heucheras and hostas, are also invaluable.

Evergreens are natural choices for container culture, because they provide something to look at for 12 months of the year. The more seasons of interest a plant can supply, the better: compact evergreens that flower and produce berries, such as skimmias, for example, make supreme container candidates.

Size and vigor

Avoid vigorous shrubs and climbing plants because they will quickly outgrow their containers and need to be transplanted elsewhere in the garden.

Above: This ingenious collection of square containers in various heights can be shunted together and rearranged to achieve a constantly changing display.

Right: Grasses and other perennials – such as hostas and heucheras – grown chiefly for their leaves provide color and interest over a long period.

However, if you have access to or can afford very large containers – at least 30 inches wide and deep – many will survive for a few years at least. Even small trees will grow in pots that are big enough, although compared to the potential lifespan of the tree, this is often a short-term arrangement. Otherwise, opt instead for dwarf or slower-growing species – many large shrubs have forms or cultivars that are more compact in habit.

Permanent or temporary?

That said, the vast majority of plants are happy in containers and can be divided into two groups: permanent structural plants and plants that provide a temporary splash of color and interest. The permanent group includes trees, shrubs, climbing plants and perennials grown for their foliage appeal. The temporaries include annuals, biennials, perennials grown mainly for their flowers, tender perennials and bulbs.

Soil and conditions

Containers also offer the solution to growing plants you otherwise could not consider. If your soil is alkaline, for instance, plants like rhododendrons and camellias that need acidic soil will not flourish unless planted in pots of an ericaceous (lime-free) soil mix. Equally, plants that may be too vigorous for the open garden, such as mint, can be kept under control in pots.

Finally, just as in the garden, it is important to choose plants that will live together and enjoy the same conditions as well as simply look good together. It therefore pays to invest a little time and effort in ensuring that the plants you choose are exactly right for the purpose.

Left: Evergreens such as skimmias and ivies provide permanent all-year-round interest while temporary flowering plants add seasonal color.

Below: An elevated row of clipped box (*Buxus*) spheres draws the eye, achieving a simple, classy formality while also providing permanent structure.

Siting and grouping containers

Among the many advantages of growing plants in containers is the opportunity this provides to cultivate, side by side, species that require different soil conditions and nutrient levels. Consequently, it is possible to achieve combinations and groupings that would be totally unrealistic in the garden border. By understanding their specific needs and caring for them accordingly, plants such as damp-loving hostas can be grown cheek to cheek with drought-tolerant succulents, and acid-loving rhododendrons beside lime-loving clematis.

Above: A plain wall or fence can be adorned using pots and baskets. Here a trio of terracotta pots is backed by old roof tiles and filled with cheery pansies.

Arrange and rearrange

A great plus is the fact that most containers can be moved around easily, allowing you to rearrange them – in the same way you would move ornaments and furniture around in the house. Also, plants that are past their best can be removed from a collection of individual pots without causing disruption and replaced with something new.

This is not to say that all potted plants have to be displayed in a group setting: a well-chosen architectural plant in a single pot, for example, can be a striking feature in its own right, especially as a focal point within a wider vista.

Filling gaps

Containers are also a good way of brightening up parts of the garden where most plants have difficulty growing, such as paved areas or very dry patches at the foot of a high hedge. They can also be used to fill temporary gaps in borders or even left in position permanently. You can either "cheat" and hide the pot itself among the other plants, or make a full-blown feature of it.

Borders can be improved in this way, because the contrast of color and texture provided by a terracotta pot, say, will highlight the plants that are growing in and around it. Many pots, including elegant olive jars and classical urns, are extremely attractive in their own right and can be sited as focal points without even holding plants.

Formal or informal?

Collections of pots and other containers can either be arranged informally or used in a more regimented fashion.

A row of box (*Buxus*) or lavenders (*Lavandula*) in matching pots flanking a flight of steps or equally spaced around a symmetrical pool, for instance, will create a strong formal image. In contrast, potted herbs and tender perennials in an assortment of terracotta containers create a jumbly, haphazard feel.

Right: Dwarf daffodils, primroses, snowdrops and irises summon up the essence of spring and are used to liven up a dull corner.

Far right: Don't plant just a hanging basket, plant a matching window box as well. Themed collections of containers are guaranteed to draw and delight the eye.

Below right: Bold pots with a strong architectural presence are accentuated by a selection of handsome plants, creating a stunning focal point.

In fact, pots can add atmosphere to any setting, and by choosing the appropriate plants, containers and accessories, you can achieve whatever mood you like, be it romantic and flowery or sharp and contemporary. You do not even need numerous containers to turn your vision into reality – just a handful of well-chosen ones is enough to get the right look.

The right background

Backgrounds can often be as important as the pots themselves and will make a major contribution to the overall effect. The right background can make a container look ten times better, while the wrong background may numb its effectiveness almost completely.

For example, pots filled with flowers always stand out better if the background plants are plain and unfussy, while variegated plants need a similarly simple backdrop – a selection of variegated leaves set against each other often gives a messy, cluttered impression.

Fences, walls and screens all make excellent foils for plants in containers, but once again you will need to match the plants to their setting and vice versa to create a pleasing effect.

Enjoy your plants

Finally, and most importantly, make use of the opportunity containers present for siting particularly pleasing plants close to seating areas, paths, windows, doors and other places where they can really be appreciated to the fullest extent.

Throwing open a window and catching the scent of flamboyant lilies (*Lilium*) or sitting out on a warm summer evening with friends and inhaling the heady perfume of sweet peas (*Lathyrus odoratus*) makes any effort involved in your garden worthwhile.

Planting and aftercare

The key to success with containers lies in understanding the needs of the plants that grow in them. A potted plant is, in effect, no different than an animal kept as a pet because it is ill-equipped to fend for itself and therefore relies upon its keeper for all its care.

Growing plants in containers gives you the opportunity to provide them with the precise growing conditions they prefer. You can tailor the soil mix and degree of watering and feeding to suit specific plants – effectively, you can create a controlled microclimate.

Soil mixes

The array of soil mixes for sale can be confusing, but there are really only three main types, each of which can be adapted to suit specific plants. For instance, extra grit or sharp sand can be added for plants that require good drainage, while an extra helping of water-storing granules will aid those that prefer moister conditions. Do not be tempted to use ordinary garden soil in place of specially prepared mixes, as you will risk importing pests and diseases.

Loam-based potting soil

Loam- or soil-based mixes are the best choice for plants that are intended to remain in their containers long term. They hold nutrients for a much longer period and are heavier and more substantial than soilless mixes. They are ideal for trees, shrubs, climbers and

Left: A good quality, general purpose potting mix ensures a healthy, long-lasting display like this summery show.

hardy perennials. They are also useful in windy locations where pots filled with a soilless mixture would blow over.

Soilless potting soil
Based on peat or peat substitutes such as coir, soilless mixes are the most widely used. Termed "general purpose" or "multi-purpose," they are ideal for short-term plants such as annuals and bulbs. Specific hanging basket and container mixes are also available and generally include a wetting agent to aid watering. Soilless mixes are lightweight and dry out more quickly than soil-based types. Most contain enough nutrients for the first six weeks of use, after which supplementary feeding will be necessary.

Ericaceous (lime-free) potting soil
Lime-hating plants that require an acidic soil, such as rhododendrons, camellias and pieris, must be planted in an ericaceous (acidic, lime-free) mix in order to flourish. Acidic mixes can also be used to ensure blue-flowered hydrangeas keep their color – in ordinary soil they will revert to pink.

Mulches
Any method that helps to conserve moisture in containers and cuts down on watering is worth considering. Mulching – covering the surface of the soil mix with a layer of a moisture-conserving material – is not only practical but can also be very decorative.

   Organic mulches such as bark chips or cocoa shells will slowly decompose into the mix. Inorganic materials such as gravel, slate, pebbles, recycled glass and marbles are permanent and, used creatively, can enhance the overall appearance of a container planting.

planting

Planting in containers is very simple, but there are a few basic guidelines that will ensure success.

Planting a pot, trough or window box

1 Place a layer of broken clay pots or coarse gravel over the drainage holes in the base of the container to prevent waterlogging.

2 Mix a few water-storing granules with the soil mix if necessary and fill the container half to three-quarters full with potting soil, depending on the size of the plants you are using.

3 Once you are happy with the positions of the plants, tip them out of their pots and plant them. Fill in around them with more soil mix, making sure they are not buried too deeply.

4 Firm the mix around the plants, push in some plugs of controlled-release fertilizer and water thoroughly.

5 For containers where the surface of the compost will be exposed for any length of time, apply a moisture-conserving mulch of bark, slate, pebbles, marbles or other similar decorative material.

Planting a hanging basket
Planting a wire or plastic mesh hanging basket takes more patience and a little longer than planting other containers.

1 Stand the basket on an empty pot for stability and place a liner inside. Moss, cocoa fiber and similar materials can be built up in layers; with other liners, such as plastic, foam or molded fiber, you will need to cut holes if you wish to plant through the sides of the basket.

2 Add some soil mix and push small plants through the sides of the basket from the inside out. It is important not to damage the roots, because this can cause a check in growth.

3 Build up the planting in the basket in two or three layers, adding more plants and soil mix as you go. Add water-storing granules to the mix at this stage, if required.

4 Plant the top of the basket with a central, upright-growing plant and put trailers or semi-trailers around the edges. Make sure that the level of the mix in the center of the basket is slightly lower than that around the edges. This will help to direct water to the roots of the plants.

5 Add fertilizer plugs and water thoroughly. Stand the completed basket in a sheltered place to allow the plants to establish for a couple of weeks before hanging up in its final position.

INTRODUCTION

Right: This space-saving planter has individual pockets that drain freely and are ideal for growing herbs and alpine plants that resent being too wet.

Below: Drainage in this wooden trough of vegetables and flowers is aided by matching "feet" that raise it off the ground and allow excess water to drain away.

Opposite: In frost-prone areas, young plants and those that are not reliably hardy can be over-wintered in a greenhouse, conservatory or even a cool room indoors.

Watering

Correct watering is crucial to the success of container gardens. You cannot rely on rain to provide sufficient moisture, because the top surface of most containers will be covered by a dense canopy of foliage that even a heavy downpour may not penetrate. Unlike those in the open ground, containerized plants cannot search for moisture beyond the confines of their pot. In addition, the mix in containers tends to dry out faster than most garden soils. Even in winter, evergreens will often need watering because they lose moisture through their leaves due to drying winds.

The best way to water a container is with a watering can, removing the rose and directing the water at the plant roots. Pour slowly so that the water soaks into the mix rather than running off, and repeat until the roots are saturated.

Another effective way to water potted plants is to stand them in water-filled saucers so that they can draw up as much moisture as they need. Tip away any excess, because most plants resent standing in water. Small containers that have dried out can be submerged in water until they stop producing bubbles.

In summer, it may be necessary to water some containers twice a day, particularly those filled with fast-maturing temporary plants such as half-hardy annuals. This depends entirely on their position, the weather and the type of container. On a hot day, a terracotta pot in full sun will dry out much more quickly than a plastic pot in half-shade. Water in the morning or the evening to reduce evaporation.

Watering aids

Various products are available that are designed to aid watering plants in containers. Water-storing polymers are small granules that swell on contact with water. You can mix small amounts with the soil. They hold moisture and are helpful in instances where an occasional watering may be missed – they are *not* a substitute for proper watering. Wetting agents work in a slightly different way, allowing you to re-wet dried-out soil mix more easily.

Irrigation systems

Various watering systems are available, including "drip" systems that slowly and thoroughly water the plant roots. These are ideal for hanging baskets and large collections of pots, because you can simply turn on the tap and leave the system to get on with it for a measured length of time.

Drainage

Good drainage is as important as watering. It is just as easy for a plant to suffer from waterlogging as from drought. Ensure that there are adequate drainage holes in the base of the container and place a layer of coarse grit or broken pots over them. Wherever possible, stand your containers on bricks or special "feet" to ensure that the drainage holes do not become clogged.

Feeding

Every time you water, nutrients are washed through the soil mix, so you need to replace them on a regular basis. Controlled-release fertilizers can be added in the form of "plugs" to release nutrients gradually into the mix. These are ideal for long-term plantings, but it is best to feed temporary displays with a soluble or liquid fertilizer that is diluted and watered in. For flowers, choose a

high-potash fertilizer and for foliage select one that is high in nitrogen.

General care

To keep your plants in good condition, a little routine care may be necessary. This includes removing dead flowers to prevent the plant diverting its energies into seed production. Many plants also benefit from pinching out, pruning and training to ensure compact, bushy growth.

Winter protection

Many otherwise hardy plants are more susceptible to frost and other adverse weather conditions when grown in

containers. During prolonged spells of very cold weather the roots of evergreens, for example, can freeze. Because they cannot draw up water, the plants will suffer as if in a drought.

Move plants that are not hardy to a frost-free place in winter. Evergreens need somewhere light, but dormant plants can be put in a dark place such as a shed and protected with row cover material or bubble wrap.

Move plants that must remain outside to a sheltered spot, perhaps protected by a large shrub, and insulate the roots with straw or bubble wrap. Alternatively, "plunge" small pots into the garden soil.

Problem solving

Plants in containers are just as susceptible to pests and diseases as those growing in the garden, but they are generally easier to keep an eye on and consequently easier to treat. If spotted early enough, most pests can be controlled quite satisfactorily, although the majority of diseases are easier to prevent than to cure.

Pests

Vine weevil

The larvae of vine weevils are a serious threat to container plants. The tiny off-white, brown-headed grubs eat through the roots of many plants, especially those with fleshy roots or crowns such as heucheras and cyclamen. Effective methods of control include biological nematodes and chemical controls that can be watered on or included in the soil mix.

Snails

Slugs find most of their food at ground level, but snails climb. Growing plants in containers gives you a head start, but snails will find them eventually. Besides proprietary slug baits, various methods can be used to combat snails. These range from attaching a ring of copper tape under the pot rims to sinking beer or bran traps nearby as a fatal distraction.

Aphids

These pests are sap-sucking insects that cause distorted growth and spread viral infections among plants. If noticed early, affected shoots and leaves can be removed quickly; alternatively, careful use of an insecticide will deal with them effectively. Spraying with horticultural soft soap, an insecticide based on

pyrethrum, or encouraging beneficial insects, such as hoverflies, that feed on aphids, are more environmentally friendly options.

Caterpillars

Plants such as dahlias, nasturtiums and lettuces can be devoured almost overnight by caterpillars. Small numbers can simply be picked off, leaf and all, but use contact insecticide for heavy infestations.

Whitefly

In warm weather whiteflies can affect plants growing outdoors, because they multiply rapidly in dry conditions. Treat with a systemic insecticide or try "companion planting" using French marigolds (*Tagetes*), which repel whitefly.

Diseases

Gray mold (botrytis)

Thriving in damp conditions where air circulation is poor, botrytis is a fungus that shows up as a furry gray mold on leaves and stems. Remove affected parts and dispose of them carefully, before spraying with a systemic fungicide to prevent the mold from spreading. Destroy badly affected plants.

Powdery mildew

Usually apparent on the upper surface of the leaf, powdery mildew appears as white spots that gradually spread. Keep plants well watered, pick off leaves at the first signs of the problem, and pick up and destroy affected fallen leaves to prevent outbreaks. If necessary, spray with a contact fungicide.

Rust

Difficult to control, rusts show as rusty-brown pustules on the undersides of leaves with corresponding yellow spots above. Remove the worst-affected leaves and spray the remainder with a fungicide.

Types of control

Contact chemicals

Contact insecticides work when they come into direct contact with pests, either when pests crawl over a treated surface or are hit directly by a spray. Contact fungicides kill germinating fungal spores and may halt or slow down the spread of infection.

Systemic chemicals

Absorbed into all parts of the plant, systemic insecticides are particularly effective against sap-sucking insects but have less control over pests that chew leaves. Systemic fungicides kill fungi within the tissues of the plant itself.

Biological controls

This type of control involves introducing the pests' natural enemies and is generally specific to one type of pest. With one or two exceptions, they are only effective in the controlled environment of a greenhouse or conservatory and should not be used in conjunction with chemicals that may harm them.

Other organic controls

Organic controls are non-chemical methods of combating pests and diseases. They include trapping nocturnal pests by providing upturned pots for them to hide in by day or using plants such as hyssop (*Hyssopus officinalis*), garlic (*Allium sativum*) or chives (*A. schoenoprasum*) to repel specific pests.

Planted pots

Pots are the most universal containers. They are available in every shape, size and style imaginable and there are types to suit every garden, every gardener and every budget. They can be grouped together and rearranged endlessly, allowing you to experiment with color combinations and foliage textures. Should you move, you can even load them up and take them with you.

Filled with annual flowers, pots create the most transient of all gardens. However, when planted with structural evergreens, they can provide an imposing air of permanence. By relying on permanently potted plants as a basic framework, tubs of temporary color can be used to ensure an ever-changing, always interesting, year-round tapestry of leaves and flowers.

Pots can also be used to overcome problems posed by difficult sites. These can range from shallow stony ground where many plants will struggle, to walls where climbing plants would look wonderful but where there is no soil at the base in which to grow them. In these situations, planting in pots can provide an instant solution.

All types of plants can grow in pots, from productive fruit, vegetables and herbs to diminutive alpines and tactile grasses. Grown in this way, tender plants can be moved indoors easily to overwinter somewhere sheltered, and varieties requiring sharp, free-draining soil can be accommodated even though the soil in your garden may be heavy clay.

Accessorized with complementary props and ornaments, a group of pots can be used to conjure up a special theme or mood. Whether you desire a tropical paradise, a coastal haven or a wildflower meadow, an arrangement of pots can turn such dreams into a scaled-down reality.

Winter sunshine

This cheery collection of evergreens is sure to brighten even the dullest winter day. All the plants are widely available and have been chosen for their reliability, ease of culture and ability to provide interest and color throughout the winter. The light blue glazed pot adds extra vibrancy to the display.

If you grow them in a large enough pot, these plants will live happily together for two or three years. Alternatively, dig them up at the end of their first spring and pot up into individual containers or plant them in the garden.

The centerpiece here is *Choisya ternata* 'Sundance', a golden-leaved form of the Mexican orange blossom that thrives in light shade. In contrast, *Leucothoe* 'Zeblid' (syn. *L.* Scarletta), a small to medium-sized shrub that

requires ericaceous (lime-free) soil, has leaves that are dark red-purple when young, turn green with age and, in winter, color to bronze. A good alternative is *L. fontanesiana* 'Rainbow', with leaves that are mottled cream and pink. *Skimmia japonica* subsp. *reevesiana*, with its clusters of red berries and leathery leaves, further enhances the scene. As a bonus, in spring all three shrubs bear white flowers.

To complete the picture and dress the edges of the pot we have used *Hedera helix* 'Goldchild', a handsome golden-variegated ivy.

Although only the leucothoe is strictly acid-loving, the skimmia will also benefit from being planted in ericaceous soil, and the choisya and the ivy will thrive, too. Site this container in a lightly shaded, sheltered position close to the house where it can be readily admired.

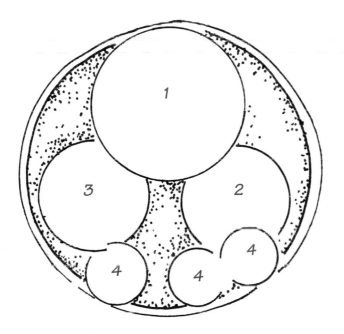

planting key

1 *Choisya ternata* 'Sundance'
2 *Leucothoe* 'Zeblid'
3 *Skimmia japonica* subsp. *reevesiana*
4 *Hedera helix* 'Goldchild'

plant close-up

SKIMMIAS

With their glossy green leaves, white flowers and clusters of red berries, skimmias are invaluable evergreens for winter and spring containers.

In most cases, you will need to grow a male plant in close proximity to the female plants in order for the latter to bear berries. However, *Skimmia japonica* subsp. *reevesiana* (pictured above) carries male and female flowers on the same plant and produces berries without the aid of a mate. Slowly forming a neat dome-shaped shrub, like most other skimmias it will happily live out most of its life in a container.

Also worthy of note, *S. japonica* 'Rubella' is a compact male clone with particularly handsome leaves and clusters of deep pink buds that appear in autumn and open pure white in spring. Among the females, *S.* 'Nymans' and *S.* 'Veitchii' (syn. *S.* 'Foremanii') produce reliable crops of large berries, and *S.* 'Fructu Albo' is an uncommon white-fruited form. Grown mainly for its white spring flowers, *S.* 'Fragrans' is highly perfumed, while *S. x confusa* 'Kew Green' produces particularly large flowerheads; both are males.

Tough and winter hardy, skimmias thrive in deep humus-rich soil in full sun or light to deep shade – they will usually struggle in a very hot position. Their tolerance of pollution makes skimmias good for urban gardens, and they also cope well with salt spray in coastal areas. Plant these useful shrubs in ericaceous soil mix and make sure they do not dry out in summer.

Top topiary

Shrubs and conifers clipped into ornamental shapes, known as topiary, are guaranteed conversation pieces and always fashionable. The clipped and trained specimens at garden centers usually carry a hefty price tag, but they are worth it. You are paying not just for the plant, but for years of training and expert care.

If you can't afford ready-grown ornamental shapes, then why not do it yourself? Tackle the job with a sense of fun and you'll be surprised at what you can achieve. Some specimens will take many years to perfect, but simple shapes such as balls and pyramids can be created relatively quickly.

Of course, the speed of growth will depend on the type of plant you use. Evergreens are best, and the

number one topiary plant is box (*Buxus*). Its tiny leaves and resilient nature make it ideal for small-scale topiary. Yew (*Taxus*), holly (*Ilex*) and bay (*Laurus nobilis*) are also popular, but if you want to see results much more quickly, consider the box-leaved honeysuckle (*Lonicera nitida*) or cypress conifers such as *Cupressus macrocarpa*. In fact, almost any evergreen has potential in the hands of a budding topiarist.

If you are really in a hurry, the easiest and speediest form of green sculpture involves trailing evergreen climbers, such as ivies (*Hedera*), over a wire frame. You can buy ready-made frames or make your own using galvanized wire.

In winter, topiary sculptures really come into their own, providing an interesting focus when the branches of deciduous shrubs and the ground itself are stripped bare.

Ivies (*Hedera*) are among the most versatile plants you could wish for. They are evergreen, tough, available in a range of leaf colors and, above all, tolerant of occasional neglect.

The smaller-leaved kinds are especially suitable for training along wires and on frames to form topiary shapes, and are also useful trailing plants for the edges of pots or hanging baskets. The many forms and cultivars of the common ivy (*H. helix*) are among the few hardy plants that can also be treated as indoor specimens, reveling in the humidity of kitchens and bathrooms.

Each lime-green and cream leaf of *H. helix* 'Chester' has a distinctive dark green central blotch, while those of *H. helix* 'Eva' are gray-green with generous creamy margins. *H. helix* 'Luzii' has medium-sized leaves speckled with cream. The vigorous stems of *H. helix* 'Pedata', the bird's foot ivy, are clothed with dark green, narrowly elongated leaves. For a splash of bright yellow choose *H. helix* 'Buttercup', although it needs careful siting because the foliage turns lime-green in shade and may scorch in full sun. One of the best variegated ivies is *H. helix* 'Goldchild' (pictured above), with leaves broadly margined with yellow.

Ivies respond well to trimming. Overgrown plants can be pruned back severely, repotted and fed to rejuvenate them.

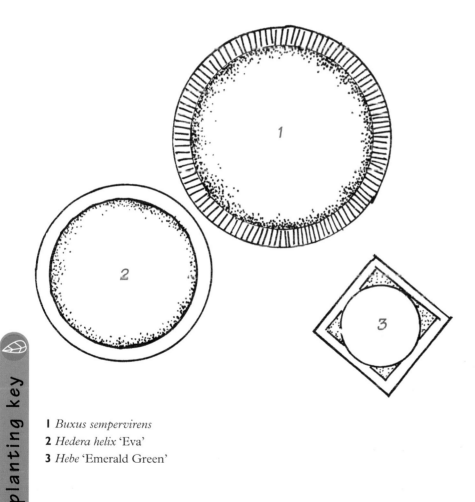

planting key

1 *Buxus sempervirens*
2 *Hedera helix* 'Eva'
3 *Hebe* 'Emerald Green'

Into the woods

Conjuring up the unique atmosphere of a woodland in early spring, this collection of hellebores, dwarf narcissi, primroses and pulmonarias has a magical presence.

Lenten roses (*Helleborus orientalis* and *H. × hybridus*) are among the most aristocratic of flowers, opening their saucer-shaped blooms in sumptuous shades ranging from velvety purple to creamy white. In contrast, the stinking hellebore (*H. foetidus*) is grown chiefly for its handsome dark green, fingered leaves, although the clusters of bell-shaped, pale apple-green flowers provide extra interest. Both look good in this wide terracotta pot.

Filling out the middle ground, *Narcissus* 'February Gold', a reliable dwarf daffodil, pokes its yellow trumpets through the foliage of the hellebores. A drift of pale yellow primroses (*Primula vulgaris*) and an underplanting of silver-leaved *Pulmonaria saccharata* Argentea Group with blue flowers help to create a tiered planting effect.

Pulmonarias are excellent perennials: not only do they bear clusters of brightly colored flowers in shades of pink, blue, red and white, but most of them also have foliage that is splashed or spotted with silver or white. The leaves are an appropriate foil for the blooms and are very attractive in their own right.

The woodland theme is accentuated by twigs or branches placed artistically among the plants, with a few fallen leaves or a handful of pine cones laid on the soil surface. Add a moss-covered log or stone and a few individually potted primroses or daffodils to enhance the picture.

PRIMULAS

Primroses (*Primula vulgaris*) and polyanthus (*P.* Polyanthus Group) are cheery and long-lasting spring flowers. Blooming for weeks on end, they are a good choice for containers and will thrive in sun or light shade.

Not all are brash and colorful; many are more subtle and invite close inspection to appreciate their beauty. For example, the Gold-laced Group of polyanthus (pictured above) — hybrids of various primula species that bear a cluster of flowers atop stout stems — have petals finely embroidered with a lacy edging of golden yellow.

Double primroses bear rosette-like flowers in every shade from deep claret-red through to cream and white. Partner them with tulips for a classy display. Plants derived from *P.* 'Wanda' are similar to primroses but are generally daintier with colors that are more intense, tending toward violet-purple and garnet-red.

Auriculas (*P. auricula*) are suited to growing in a cold greenhouse where their exquisite, richly colored blooms and often white-mealy foliage are protected from wind and rain.

To keep primulas in good order, remove faded flowers and yellowing leaves and keep them well watered. After flowering, large clumps can be lifted, split and replanted. Sow seed in late spring or early summer for plants that will flower the following spring.

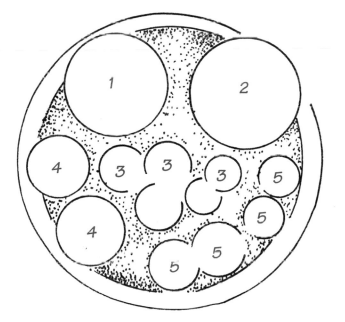

planting key

1 *Helleborus orientalis* white seedling
2 *Helleborus foetidus*
3 *Narcissus* 'February Gold'
4 *Pulmonaria saccharata* Argentea Group
5 *Primula vulgaris*

Spring is here: I

Flowering bulbs are the colorful mainstay of most spring containers. With careful planning, you can enjoy a succession of flowers from late winter through to early summer.

However, the individual flowers are all fleeting, so it makes sense to grow each variety in a separate pot and plunge them in groups into larger containers. As one pot fades, it can be removed easily and replaced by another that is just about to bloom.

Skimmia japonica 'Rubella' provides a stable backdrop for a constantly changing display. *Primula* 'Miss Indigo', a deep blue double primrose with white-edged petals, and deep pink-flowered *Erica carnea* 'Myretoun Ruby', a tough winter-flowering heather, fill the foreground for

the first half of the spring. *Hedera helix* 'Glacier', with leaves variegated creamy white, softens the edge of the container.

The earliest bulbs to flower are snowdrops (*Galanthus*) and yellow-flowered aconites (*Eranthis*), although in this collection they have already been replaced by later-blooming crocuses such as *C. tommasinianus* 'Whitewell Purple' and reticulata irises like *I.* 'Harmony', which are joined by the pale china-blue stars of glory-of-the-snow (*Chionodoxa luciliae* Gigantea Group). Yellow-and-orange *Narcissus* 'Jetfire', one of the most striking of all dwarf narcissus, and *N.* 'Topolino', with creamy-white petals and yellow trumpets, add height and a strong vertical axis in the back row.

To complete the display, *Tulipa humilis* Violacea Group is tucked in where it can open its lavender flowers in the warmth of the sun to reveal bright yellow centers.

Better equipped to cope with adverse weather conditions than their taller cousins, dwarf daffodils, or narcissus, are perfectly suited to container culture.

Often blooming a few weeks ahead of the taller varieties, dwarf narcissus range in height from 4 to 12 inches. Of particular value are multi-headed kinds such as *Narcissus* 'Tête-à-tête', an early-flowering variety. Daintier and later-flowering, *N.* 'Hawera' (pictured above) carries up to five canary-yellow flowers per stem and each bulb may produce several stems. The slender stems of *N.* 'Jumblie' rise only 7 inches high before the small clusters of strongly reflexed, golden-yellow blooms begin to open.

N. 'Pipit' is a sweetly scented lemon-and-white cultivar, while the lemon-yellow trumpets of *N.* 'Jack Snipe', with white backs on the petals, are exceptionally long-lasting. The nodding, lemon-yellow blooms of *N.* 'Liberty Bells' are elegantly poised and the enchanting creamy-white flowers of *N.* 'Thalia' stand out. Taller and more obviously daffodil-like are the descriptively named *N.* 'February Gold' and *N.* 'February Silver'.

Plant bulbs in early autumn. Cover with soil mix to 1½ times their depth and space so that the bulbs are nearly touching. Remove faded flowers and allow the leaves to die naturally for at least six weeks after flowering before removing them. A high-potash fertilizer boosts flowering potential for the following year.

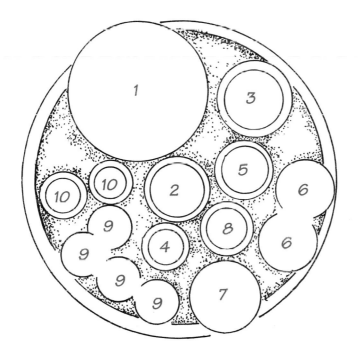

planting key

1 *Skimmia japonica* 'Rubella'
2 *Narcissus* 'Jetfire'
3 *Narcissus* 'Topolino'
4 *Iris* 'Harmony'
5 *Tulipa humilis* Violacea Group
6 *Erica carnea* 'Myretoun Ruby'
7 *Hedera helix* 'Glacier'
8 *Chionodoxa luciliae*
   Gigantea Group
9 *Primula* 'Miss Indigo'
10 *Crocus tommasinianus*
   'Whitewell Purple'

Spring is here: 2

Moving on a month or so, the early spring bulbs will have flowered and gone. This next selection extends the flowering period into the second half of spring and even beyond. It is entirely up to you whether you opt for a haphazard mixture or decide to choose a carefully executed color scheme.

Dwarf tulips are the elegant, cheery backbone of this group. As spring progresses, the skimmia opens its starry blooms and the primroses and heathers of the scheme on pages 28–29 are replaced by forget-me-nots (*Myosotis sylvatica* 'Blue Ball') with pale blue flowers to accompany the kaleidoscope of tulips.

The first of the tulips to flower is *Tulipa linifolia* Batalinii Group 'Bright Gem', a 14-inch-high beauty

with goblets of apricot-yellow flushed with orange and shaded bronze at the base. Brightest, glowing red *T. praestans* 'Fusilier' offers exceptionally good value because of its multi-flowered stems, while *T.* 'Pinocchio' holds its strawberry-pink, creamy-margined blooms proudly above neat clumps of darkly striped leaves.

The very unusual orange flowers of *T.* 'Prinses Irene' are shaded purple at the base of each petal and held aloft on slender stems. *T.* 'Sweetheart' forms a breathtaking contrast with its cool, lemon-yellow petals that fade to ivory-white at the tips.

Taller, late-flowering tulips can see you through to the end of spring. Once they have faded, replace the forget-me-nots with violas and add some pots of ornamental onions (*Allium*) to extend the show well into summer.

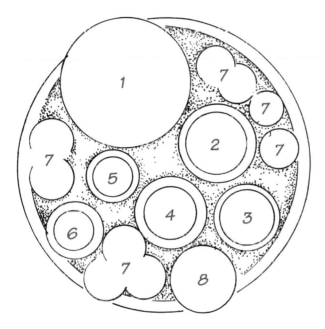

planting key

1 *Skimmia japonica* 'Rubella'
2 *Tulipa* 'Prinses Irene'
3 *Tulipa* 'Pinocchio'
4 *Tulipa praestans* 'Fusilier'
5 *Tulipa* 'Sweetheart'
6 *Tulipa linifolia* Batalinii Group 'Bright Gem'
7 *Myosotis sylvatica* 'Blue Ball'
8 *Hedera helix* 'Glacier'

plant close-up

DWARF TULIPS

Of all the various kinds of tulips available, dwarfs are the most useful for containers.

Tulips thrive in well-drained soil and full sun. For the best results, plant one or two varieties a pot. Take care when using more because they can look messy and may not flower at the same time. Plant the bulbs close together in layers for a packed display – they can be almost touching. Finish off with a layer of gravel to prevent soil from splashing them.

Tulipa linifolia is a dainty variety with slender leaves and bright red blooms carried on 8-inch stems, while *T. l.* Batalinii Group 'Bronze Charm' has beautiful apricot-yellow flowers. Among the earliest to bloom are the kaufmanniana or 'water lily' tulips, so called because their large blooms open wide like water lilies. The petals of *T.* 'Giuseppe Verdi' are golden yellow on the inside and bright red edged with yellow on the outside, while the deep green leaves of *T.* 'Shakespeare' are topped by blooms that are a blend of salmon, red and yellow.

Slightly taller and later-flowering, cultivars bred from *T. fosteriana* and *T. greigii* include *T.* 'Cape Cod' (apricot-yellow striped with red), *T.* 'Corsage' (rose-pink with yellow-margined petals and maroon-shaded leaves) and (pictured above) *T.* 'Purissima' (tall, pure white).

Turn up the heat

That unique moment when the fresh tones of spring fade away to make way for the vibrancy of summer is marked by this late-spring symphony of color. Using a range of plants with bright and sunny colors will ensure a warm transition into summer – whatever the weather.

A glowing range of yellow, apricot and orange shades is supplied here by *Ranunculus* 'Accolade' and spring-flowering pansies (*Viola × wittrockiana*). *Euonymus fortunei* 'Emerald 'n' Gold', an extremely hardy dwarf evergreen, contributes to the overall glow, courtesy of its yellow-and-green variegated leaves. Dangling its trailing stems over the rim of the pot, *Hedera helix* 'Kolibri', a neat, small-leaved, creamy-white variegated ivy, rounds

off the planting. The euonymus and the ivy will look good long after the pansies and ranunculus have finished, and the sunny theme can be continued by planting yellow French marigolds (*Tagetes*) and orange pelargoniums.

Many spring-flowering pansies can be grown from seed sown the previous summer and the Ultima Series offers one of the widest color ranges of all. Here primrose, orange and apricot shades are teamed with the yellow ranunculus – which are, in effect, giant double buttercups – to achieve a radiant result. Pick off the faded pansy blooms regularly to keep them blooming well, and if they become a little straggly, trim them back.

The warm tones of weathered terracotta pots provide the base for this collection, and the effect of the main pot is mirrored by individual pots crammed with more pansies and ranunculus.

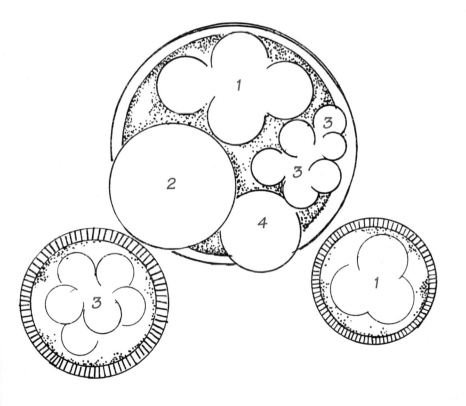

planting key

1 *Ranunculus* 'Accolade' yellow shades

2 *Euonymus fortunei* 'Emerald 'n' Gold'

3 *Viola* × *wittrockiana* Ultima Series primrose, orange and apricot shades

4 *Hedera helix* 'Kolibri'

DWARF EVERGREENS

Offering year-round interest, evergreens are excellent candidates for permanent container displays and can be kept in pots for many years.

Among the most reliable are euonymus, in particular the cultivars of *E. fortunei*. Thriving in sun or shade, most grow no more than 2 to 3 feet tall and are very hardy. All can be clipped easily to keep them within bounds. Suitable cultivars of *E. fortunei* include yellow-variegated 'Emerald 'n' Gold'; 'Emerald Gaiety', with creamy-white margins to its leaves; 'Kewensis', a tiny, prostrate green-leaved variety; 'Sunspot', with golden-centered leaves; and 'Dart's Blanket', with dark green leaves that turn bronze in autumn.

Less hardy, but still useful for pots, are hebes. The dwarf kinds are content in full sun. Tiny flowers in purple, mauve or white are borne in summer, but most dwarf hebes are grown for their attractive leaves. *H. ochracea* 'James Stirling' (pictured above) grows 18 inches high and 24 inches wide, with tiny yellow-ochre leaves. *H. pinguifolia* 'Pagei' has larger, gray leaves; *H.* 'Red Edge' has larger leaves still, each with a bold red margin. *H.* 'Youngii' (syn. *H.* 'Carl Teschner') has dark green leaves and *H. pimeloides* 'Quicksilver' has silvery-gray foliage.

Dwarf rhododendrons and summer-flowering heathers (*Calluna*) are also excellent evergreens, but require ericaceous (lime-free) soil. Winter-flowering heaths (*Erica carnea* and *E.* × *darleyensis*) are as useful and are lime tolerant.

Candy confection

Guaranteeing a summer-long display of flowers, this sweet and simple selection of sugary-pink, blue and mauve half-hardy perennials is ideal for a sunny patio.

All the plants in this quartet are sun-worshippers. The planting centers around *Argyranthemum* 'Summit Pink', which forms a bushy mound of gray-green filigree foliage that is studded with pale pink, yellow-centered daisies throughout the summer. Remove dead flowers occasionally to encourage further blooms. Tucked in on either side of the argyranthemum, *Solenopsis axillaris* has free rein to display its bright blue, starry flowers that will continue until they are caught by the first frosts.

Spearing through at the back of the pot, *Angelonia*

'Angel Mist Lavender' appears above the argyranthemum, creating a complementary backdrop with spikes of lavender-mauve blooms. Because they reach a height of 20 inches, angelonias are extremely useful in any instances where a strong vertical accent is required.

Tumbling over the front, the trailing stems of *Verbena* 'Lanai Bright Pink' bear intensely deep pink young blooms that stand out well against the blue glaze of the pot. As they age, the flowers tone down to a softer shade of pink, creating a pretty two-tone effect. The wandering habit of the verbena also ensures that it will weave its way attractively through the other plants.

All these plants are classed as half-hardy or tender. Keep them in a frost-free place through winter or discard the plants and replace them with new ones the following year.

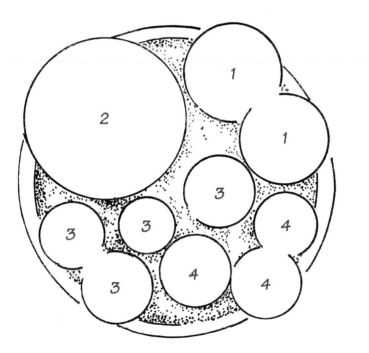

planting key

1 *Angelonia* 'Angel Mist Lavender'
2 *Argyranthemum* 'Summer Pink'
3 *Solenopsis axillaris*
4 *Verbena* 'Lanai Bright Pink'

plant close-up

VERBENAS

In recent years, plant breeders have seized on all the best qualities of various verbenas and fused them together to create a series of new varieties that are more compact and branching, considerably more free-flowering and, very importantly, mildew resistant. These new verbenas are supreme container and hanging basket plants for a sunny position. Of course, there are plenty of compact annual verbenas available as colorful seed mixtures that are ideal for bedding displays, but the trailing perennial kinds are most useful for containers.

The flattened clusters of tiny flowers vary in color from intense reds and purples, through every shade of pink, to soft lavenders and mauves. Verbenas in the Diamond Series are larger and more vigorous than most, with semi-trailing stems. *V.* 'Diamond Merci' is rich velvety red, *V.* 'Diamond Butterfly' carries heads of pale pink with darker centers and *V.* 'Diamond Rhodonit' opens vivid scarlet-red. Verbenas in the Temari Group and Lanai Series are available in a wide choice of shades. (*Verbena* 'Lanai Scarlet' is pictured above.)

Tapien verbenas, in either pink or violet, are daintier, with ferny foliage and starry five-petalled blooms. More upright in habit and strikingly different is the Splash Series. Again, the names describe the flower color and all have the appearance of having been splashed with rose-pink, purple or lavender paint.

On the prairie

Ornamental grasses are universally popular on account of their graceful forms, colorful foliage and the understated beauty of their flowers. They are especially well suited to container growing because they can be removed, divided and replanted when they become too large.

Almost all grasses – even the larger miscanthus – will grow in pots, although some will outgrow their allotted space and need repotting or dividing more quickly than others. The best grasses for containers are the low-growing, hummock-forming types such as festucas. These can be planted with other grasses or as a contrast to foliage perennials or colorful annual flowers.

The muted light brown earthenware pots used here

host a textural, "hands-on" group of grasses that you simply can't resist running your fingers through. At the back of the main pot, *Stipa tenuissima* is one of the most tactile of all grasses with slender, silky stems and flowers rising to 2 feet. Its free-seeding nature ensures you will always have plenty of plants for your other pots. To the side is *Carex flagellifera*; its gently arching blades of bronzy brown merge with the stipa and tumble over the spiky blue mound of *Festuca glauca* 'Elijah Blue', a particularly well-colored variety of Kentucky blue grass. Although it is not strictly a grass, *Ophiopogon planiscapus* 'Nigrescens', an evergreen perennial with black strap-like leaves, forms a low filler for the rest of the pot.

In the foreground pot, the pale yellow *Festuca glauca* 'Golden Toupee' stands out against the surface of the main pot.

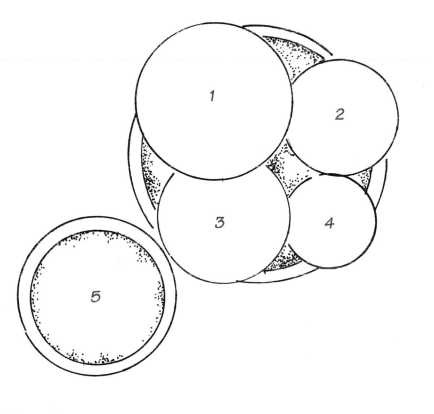

plant close-up

STIPAS

Grasses soften even the harshest landscape and introduce an air of tranquillity. The varied textures of their leaves and flowers complement natural materials such as timber or slate and their soft outlines work well against brick and stone walls.

Among the most obliging are the stipas, a group that encompasses both evergreen and deciduous species. Most of them deserve a place in every garden. Even in autumn and winter they ooze charm, with their faded flowers and leaves beautifully highlighted on frosty mornings.

Evergreen *S. arundinacea* (pictured above) forms a waterfall of dark green leaves that will dangle gracefully over the edge of a pot and become streaked with orange as summer progresses. Unlike other stipas, this species tolerates a little shade. In contrast, *S. calamagrostis* is a deciduous species that develops dense tufts of blue-green foliage topped in summer by feathery flowers of silver-purple. Both grow to around 3 feet tall.

For a plant that provides drama without being ostentatious, almost nothing is better than golden oat grass (*S. gigantea*). In summer, 6-foot stems rise from a mound of arching dark green leaves and erupt into panicles of silvery oat-like flowers that turn golden brown by autumn. Backlit by the sun, they are breathtaking.

In early spring, cut back deciduous species hard and remove dead leaves from evergreens. Split overcrowded clumps in early summer.

Purple, pink and blue

One of the most enjoyable aspects of choosing plants for containers is deciding on a color theme. A riotous mixture can look stunning, but it is usually safer to stick to a more selective color palette. Hot colors such as red, yellow and orange generally work well together, as do cooler shades including pink, white and blue. However, it can be quite surprising to see what mixes are effective.

This classic combination of colors never fails, and is set off superbly by the square galvanized steel pot. Silvers and grays are a reliable foil to any color, from rich greens to blush-pinks. Choose a sunny spot, but not the

hottest, because the steel will heat and the soil will dry out quickly.

At the back, *Pelargonium* 'Fireworks Light Pink' opens its starry blooms *en masse* on strong stems that are produced very freely. Other colors in the Fireworks Series are also worth trying, thanks to their free-flowering nature and unusually pointed, eye-catching petals.

The deep purple-red leaves of *Heuchera* 'Amethyst Myst', a hardy perennial well suited to containers, are veined with silver and are dark wine-red beneath. This coloring is accentuated by the paleness of the pelargonium and the moodiness of lavender-blue *Nemesia* 'Blue Lagoon', the final element in this mouth-watering arrangement.

As a cool alternative, try grouping *Pelargonium* 'Fireworks White' with silvery-leaved *Heucherella* 'Quicksilver' and scented white *Nemesia* 'Innocence'.

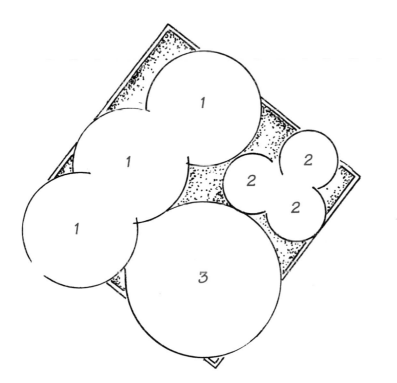

planting key

I *Pelargonium* 'Fireworks Light Pink'
2 *Nemesia* 'Blue Lagoon'
3 *Heuchera* 'Amethyst Myst'

plant close-up

NEMESIAS

If you want plants that flower all summer in a range of pretty colors, are sweetly fragrant and easy to grow, look no further than nemesias. Though not reliably hardy, these plants can be kept from year to year by overwintering them in a frost-free place and planting them out again in late spring. They can also be grown easily from cuttings taken in summer.

Nemesias produce short flower spikes that are crowded with tiny blooms in shades of pink, blue and white. Few plants are as constantly in flower, and removing spent flower spikes will promote the production of replacements. Their semi-trailing habit makes them ideal for mingling with other plants in the center of hanging baskets, or for growing around the edge of containers, where they will gently tumble while holding their heads high. Nemesias look particularly good massed in wide, shallow bowls or erupting from the top of chimney pots. Plant them with diascias or daisy-flowered *Osteospermum* for a long-running and colorful performance.

Nemesia denticulata 'Confetti', which has pink flowers and a powerful perfume, will often come through the winter outdoors if sheltered, while mauve-blue *N.* 'Blue Lagoon', a real treat of a color, and scented, pure white *N.* 'Innocence' need frost protection. Others to look for include *N. caerulea* 'Woodcote', dark blue with a yellow center and pale lavender *N.* 'Melanie' (pictured above).

On the dry side: 1

When faced with a really hot, dry spot, the obvious solution is to opt for plants that hail from countries where such conditions are normal. This aromatic container uses a mixture of plants derived from species native to the warmer parts of Europe and that are guaranteed to thrive in sunny spots.

Plants with silver or gray, narrow, hairy or fleshy leaves are the best equipped to cope with sunny, dry conditions and include a number of herbs, dwarf shrubs and perennials. Here we have chosen four of the most reliable and packed them into square terracotta pots.

Standing upright at the back of the main container, *Rosmarinus officinalis* 'Tuscan Blue' is clothed with narrow, deep green aromatic leaves that can be used to

accompany meat dishes. Bright blue flowers appear early in the year and often again in autumn. Nestling alongside it, the low gray-green mound of French lavender (*Lavandula stoechas* subsp. *pedunculata*) is topped in early summer by curious cone-shaped, purple-pink flowerheads, each crowned by two or three purple bracts that resemble wings or ears. In common with all lavenders, it has narrow aromatic leaves.

The curry plant (*Helichrysum italicum* subsp. *serotinum*) gained its common name from the unmistakable aroma of its narrow, silver leaves. Bright yellow flowers appear in summer. This pot is best sited on a patio or near a door, where you can breathe in the pungent fragrance every time you brush past.

A smaller pot with *L. × intermedia* 'Twickel Purple' – compact, with purple flowers – completes the composition.

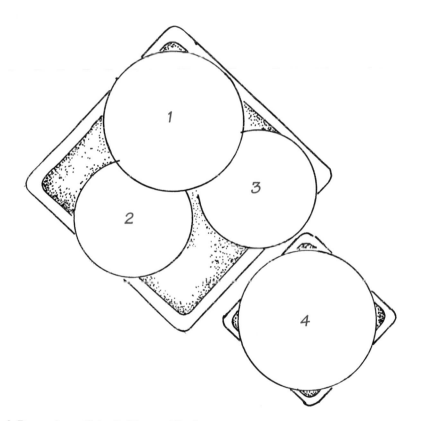

planting key

1 *Rosmarinus officinalis* 'Tuscan Blue'
2 *Lavandula stoechas* subsp. *pedunculata*
3 *Helichrysum italicum* subsp. *serotinum*
4 *Lavandula × intermedia* 'Twickel Purple'

plant close-up

MEDITERRANEAN PLANTS

Many plants of Mediterranean origin can grow successfully in more temperate climates in containers. In summer they will live quite happily outdoors on a sunny, sheltered patio, while in winter they can be insulated and protected or moved into a cool conservatory or greenhouse.

The largest group of plants reminiscent of Mediterranean locations are the pelargoniums (see page 109). Their shamelessly vibrant flowers and attractive leaves brighten many a balcony or *terrazzo*.

Among them are trailing varieties, scented-leaved types and those that, with frost protection, will reach giant proportions. The fancy-leaved varieties are especially worth growing because they offer twice the impact.

The majority of Mediterranean flowers are strongly colored; shades of vermilion, orange and hot pink are common. Brash bougainvilleas (pictured above) will liven up a whitewashed wall in shades of pink and red, and angel's trumpets (*Brugmansia*) will open their huge, pendant blooms, but are best tucked away at the back where their potentially skin-irritating leaves and stems are out of reach.

Plants with silver or gray, felty, hairy or woolly leaves, such as verbascums, also conjure up images of the Mediterranean, and the scene would not be complete without one or two palms and other bold architectural plants that cast cool shade on a hot day.

On the dry side: 2

A shady spot where the soil is dry – perhaps at the base of a wall or a high hedge – is one of the most problematic areas in a garden. If you have tried but plants simply won't grow there, try containers and sturdy plants. All the plants in this selection will tolerate occasional drying out.

An import from New Zealand, *Phormium* 'Jester' is a spiky-leaved evergreen that has proved remarkably tolerant of both drought and shade, although it will cope equally well with conditions that are the exact opposite. Its red-and-cream sword-like leaves rise here from a skirt of *Geranium macrorrhizum* 'Ingwersen's Variety', a tough, reliable perennial with aromatic leaves and numerous pale pinkish-white flowers in spring. In

autumn, the handsomely scalloped leaves develop attractive red and orange hues that persist well into winter. Few shrubs have as tough a constitution as *Euonymus fortunei* and the variety 'Emerald Gaiety' is especially obliging.

Rounding off this group is the lesser periwinkle (*Vinca minor* f. *alba* 'Gertrude Jekyll'), a tough little evergreen that produces long trailing stems clothed with rich green leaves, studded intermittently throughout spring and summer with pure white flowers. There are numerous varieties of lesser periwinkle, all of which cope with difficult soil conditions.

Although this planting is designed to survive if allowed to dry, it is still preferable to keep it well watered to encourage lush, leafy growth. With the exception of the euonymus, all the plants can be divided and replanted in spring if they become overcrowded.

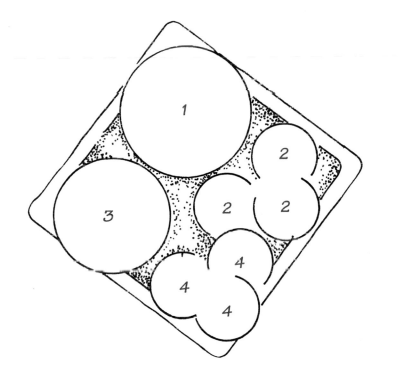

planting key

1 *Phormium* 'Jester'
2 *Geranium macrorrhizum* 'Ingwersen's Variety'
3 *Euonymus fortunei* 'Emerald Gaiety'
4 *Vinca minor* f. *alba* 'Gertrude Jekyll'

plant close-up

PLANTS FOR SHADE

Many gardeners think of shady corners as awkward spots that are difficult to furnish. However, a number of plants relish a cool, shady position tucked away from the midday sun.

If the ground is very dry, then it may be a problem. The answer is to grow a selected range of plants in containers and to rely on gravel, paving or decking to cover the ground. Choose pots that are pale in color to reflect what light there is, and add ornaments and other accessories such as pebbles or unplanted, patterned pots to add interest or create more of a focal point.

By growing shade-loving plants in pots you will be able to regulate the amount of water they receive and moist, shady conditions provide the perfect habitat for a much wider range of plants. Of the shrubs that will flourish, choose from euonymus, phormiums (both used in the container opposite), dwarf rhododendrons, pieris, *Fatsia japonica*, hydrangeas (pictured above), camellias, Japanese maples (*Acer palmatum* and *A. japonicum*) and spotted laurels (*Aucuba*). Reliable perennials in this type of situation include evergreen epimediums, lime-flowered lady's mantle (*Alchemilla mollis*), hostas in all their variety, bugle (*Ajuga*) and lungworts (*Pulmonaria*).

To keep the soil in your containers reliably damp, consider investing in a drip irrigation system that will allow you to water your plants easily and reliably at the turn of a tap.

Makes great scents

Plants are capable of exciting not just one but *all* **of the senses. Grasses and bamboos, for instance, are not only very tactile – they also rustle in a breeze, sounding very pleasant to the ear. But next to sight, the most important sense in a garden is that of smell; happily there is no shortage of scented plants.**

This carefully orchestrated trio of pots is crammed with perfumed plants that combine to delight the nose and the eyes. Place it near a path or seating area where the combination can be fully appreciated.

Lilies are among the most powerfully scented of all plants; but not all are fragrant, so check before you buy. *Lilium* 'Joy' (syn. *L.* 'Le Rêve') has large pink flowers that carry a heady scent. Compared to the other

plants in this composition their flowering period is fairly fleeting, so it is sensible to grow them in separate pots so you can remove them easily once they have faded. A mulch of gravel around the base makes a finishing touch.

Chocolate cosmos (*C. atrosanguineus*) is so called because the deep burgundy blooms have a distinct chocolate scent. It relishes a sunny spot and good drainage, as do its companions – aromatic-leaved *Pelargonium* 'Lady Plymouth' and *Heliotropium arborescens* 'Marine'. The rich purple flowers of the heliotrope have a strong scent of cooked cherries and make an attractive accompaniment to the cream-variegated leaves of the pelargonium.

The final pot in this fragrant trio is crammed with scented dwarf sweet peas (*Lathyrus odoratus* 'Patio Mix'), which are supported on short, twiggy sticks.

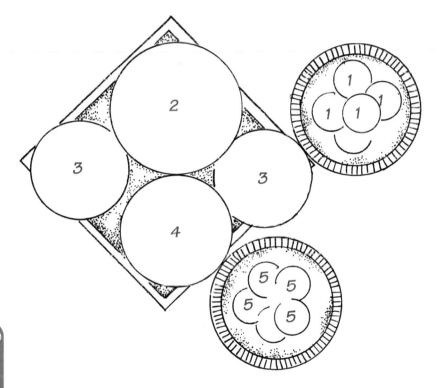

planting key

1 *Lilium* 'Joy'

2 *Cosmos atrosanguineus*

3 *Pelargonium* 'Lady Plymouth'

4 *Heliotropium arborescens* 'Marine'

5 *Lathyrus odoratus* 'Patio Mix'

plant close-up

LILIES

With an iron constitution that belies their exotic appearance, lilies are favorites for their dazzling colors, perfume and elegant height.

Of the taller species and cultivars reaching 5 feet or more, the trumpet lilies (Aurelian hybrids) have the most powerful perfume. White-flowered *Lilium regale* (pictured above) and cultivars such as *L.* Pink Perfection Group are good choices for height and perfume. Asiatic lilies do not have any scent but their stout stems and hot, bright colors make up for it.

Recently, a new race of compact patio lilies has been developed. Combining the perfume and wide color range of the taller lilies with short, strong, wind-resistant stems, they are perfect for pots. *L.* 'Fata Morgana' is a deep golden-yellow with double flowers, *L.* 'Garden Party' is white with a yellow stripe on each petal, and *L.* 'Mona Lisa' bears spotted rose-pink flowers that lighten to blush-pink at the edges.

Plant the scaly bulbs in autumn or early spring, several to a deep pot in layers, for maximum impact. Lilies like a moisture-retentive but free-draining soil and their blooms will last far longer if they are sited in light shade. Most are lime tolerant but the Oriental hybrids, among others, require an ericaceous (lime-free) mix. After flowering, feed the bulbs with a high-potash fertilizer to ensure a good display the following year. Overwinter the pots in a sheltered spot and repot in early spring using fresh soil mix.

Water barrel

There is no need to dig a pond in order to grow a range of aquatic and moisture-loving plants – less vigorous kinds, at least, can all be grown with success in water-filled containers.

Any large container that you can make watertight will do, from a large ceramic sink to an animal's drinking trough. A rustic half-barrel, sited in full sun, serves here as a handsome reservoir with a miniature red water lily (*Nymphaea* 'Pygmaea Rubra') planted in the center. A dwarf bulrush (*Typha minima*) and yellow-variegated, blue-flowered *Iris laevigata* 'Variegata' add vertical form. All are planted into plastic mesh baskets in specially prepared aquatic soil mix. In colder localities, insulate the barrel in winter by wrapping it with polyethylene

bubble wrap and foam to prevent the water from freezing solid.

As an alternative to the water lily, consider using surface-floating plants such as water hyacinths (*Eichhornia crassipes*), with lilac flowers, or the distinctive water lettuce (*Pistia stratiotes*). Both require frost protection in winter.

Houttuynia cordata 'Chameleon' comes into play to cheer up the foreground. This moisture-loving perennial will also grow in dry soils, but given a patch of damp ground it will run wild. Grow it in a pot where it is confined and you can enjoy the red, yellow, orange and green leaves with peace of mind. On the opposite side, *Hosta* 'Blue Moon' is another container favorite that is particularly at home in association with water. Its heavily ribbed blue-green leaves look especially good when seen against the dark oak of the barrel.

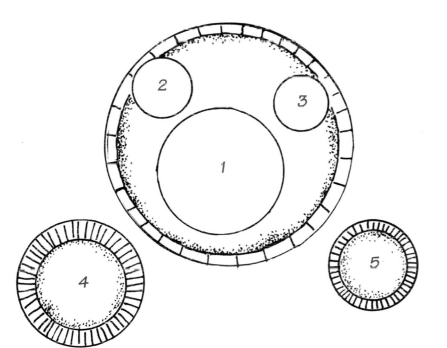

planting key

1 *Nymphaea* 'Pygmaea Rubra'
2 *Typha minima*
3 *Iris laevigata* 'Variegata'
4 *Houttuynia cordata* 'Chameleon'
5 *Hosta* 'Blue Moon'

plant close-up

WATER LILIES

Even if you garden on a balcony or in a tiny courtyard, you can achieve the tranquil effect of water lilies (*Nymphaea*), just on a smaller scale. Miniature water lilies are at home in relatively shallow water and in a container no more than 20 inches deep. They dislike moving water, so avoid the temptation to add a fountain. If you want to hear a gentle splash, set up a simple pebble fountain in an adjacent pot.

Many water lilies grow too vigorously for the average pond, spreading 6 feet or more across, but there are a handful of diminutive varieties that are perfect for containers. Choose from *N. tetragona*, a slightly fragrant variety with yellow-centered, pure white blooms, yellow-flowered *N.* 'Pygmaea Helvola' and *N.* 'Pygmaea Rubra', which bears rose-pink blooms that turn blood-red. All spread to just 18 inches across.

Water lilies grow from knobbly rhizomes and should be planted into aquatic baskets in early summer. Use a heavy, loam-based soil mix, preferably one made specifically for aquatic plants. Set the rhizomes just below the surface of the soil and cover with a layer of washed gravel. Stand the basket on a stack of bricks placed in the base of the container so that the crown of the plant is submerged to a depth of about 4 inches. Once it is established, lower the plant a little deeper into the water.

Lovely leaves

While many flowers can provide only short-term displays, plants that are grown primarily for their foliage provide interest over a much longer period – and sometimes all year round. With care, the foliage plants in this composition will look just as good in autumn as they do in spring.

At the center is the handsome honeybush (*Melianthus major*), its large, divided and serrated sea-green leaves presiding majestically over the other inhabitants. Incredibly fast-growing, it can reach a height of 6 feet in a single season. In a sheltered, sunny, frost-free spot it will remain evergreen.

Tucked below the canopy of the melianthus, × *Heucherella* 'Kimono' forms a dense mound of

handsome silver-green leaves. This useful ground-cover plant produces long sprays of tiny white flowers in spring and summer. In stark but effective contrast, the luxuriant foliage of *Heuchera* 'Chocolate Ruffles' is rich burgundy-red.

A drop of golden yellow is added to the mix courtesy of *Carex oshimensis* 'Evergold', a neat evergreen grass that develops tufts of narrow, variegated leaves. Squeezed in at the front, its arching leaves tangle with the felty silver-gray stems and foliage of *Helichrysum petiolare*. The helichrysum may not survive the winter. However, if the pot is large enough, the remaining plants should live together happily for a couple of years before they will need repotting.

As a final touch, *Heuchera* 'Cherries Jubilee' makes a compact clump of wine-red leaves topped with sprays of bright red flowers in a smaller pot.

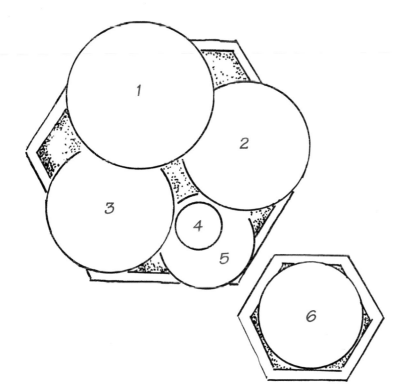

planting key

1 *Melianthus major*
2 × *Heucherella* 'Kimono'
3 *Heuchera* 'Chocolate Ruffles'
4 *Carex oshimensis* 'Evergold'
5 *Helichrysum petiolare*
6 *Heuchera* 'Cherries Jubilee'

plant close-up

HEUCHERAS

Cherished for their show of fancy foliage, heucheras are hardy perennials that deserve a place in every garden. Plum-purple, chocolate-brown and wine-red are just some of the delicious shades of their leaves. Some have marbled or cream-splashed foliage and display a subtle variation in leaf shape.

Heucheras thrive in full sun or very light shade and soil that retains some moisture yet drains freely in winter. Although the leaves of most heucheras are their primary attraction, all produce sprays of tiny white, pink or red flowers that rise elegantly above the leaves in early summer. In a frost-free spot, they remain evergreen, providing winter interest.

H. 'Chocolate Ruffles' lives up to its name with loosely crinkled leaves in a deep chocolate shade. *H.* 'Ebony and Ivory' bears flowers of pure white above dark foliage, and *H.* 'Fireworks' explodes into salmon-pink bloom. The purplish leaves of both *H.* 'Amethyst Myst' and *H.* 'Can-can' (pictured above) are delicately veined with silver. *H.* 'Pewter Moon' has gray-marbled leaves with deep pink undersides, and the cream-and green leaves of *H.* 'Snow Storm' accentuate the red flowers. A hybrid between heuchera and tiarella, *Heuchera* x *Heucherella* 'Burnished Bronze' has pink flowers above bronze-red scalloped leaves.

The fleshy rootstocks of heucheras are a target for vine weevil grubs, but they are otherwise largely unaffected by pests or diseases.

In the shade

Many plants grown for their foliage are quite tolerant of shady conditions, although color and variegation often become less pronounced in shade. In this foliage group we have opted for a variety of green fern leaves but spiced them up with a couple of hostas and a bold-leafed tiarella.

Ferns are one of the best groups of plants for shade, their soft, feathery leaves unfurling in a variety of shapes and sizes. Here, *Dryopteris filix-mas* 'Crispa Cristata' pushes up its 2-foot crested fronds to create a backdrop to the other inhabitants. Forming tight clumps, the delicate fronds of *D. erythrosora* are copper-tinted when young and make a fitting foil to the short, fresh green, lacy fronds of *Athyrium filix-*

femina 'Frizelliae', an unusual lady fern.

Hostas also make superb subjects for pots, where they are less likely to be targeted by slugs and snails. They enjoy the same moist, shady conditions as ferns, but are also happy in full sun.

Their handsome foliage is infinitely varied, from diminutive, green-leaved ground covers to extra-large leaved golden or glaucous-blue varieties. Statuesque *H.* 'Snowden' has medium-sized leaves on tall stalks that are joined in summer by slender stems carrying white, bell-shaped flowers. Forming a daintier clump of yellow-margined leaves, *H.* 'Golden Tiara' dresses the foreground.

Grown for its unusually marked leaves and foamy flowers, *Tiarella* 'Iron Butterfly' bulks up this leafy show in a separate, matching pot where it will bloom for weeks.

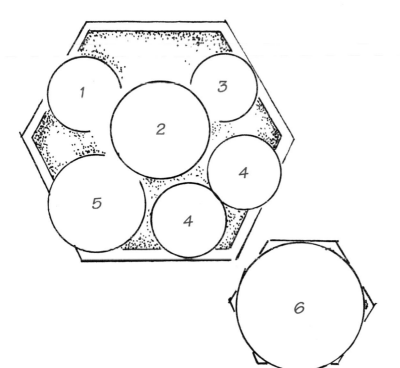

planting key

1 *Dryopteris filix-mas* 'Crispa Cristata'
2 *Hosta* 'Snowden'
3 *Dryopteris erythrosora*
4 *Athyrium filix-femina* 'Frizelliae'
5 *Hosta* 'Golden Tiara'
6 *Tiarella* 'Iron Butterfly'

plant close-up

FERNS

From the moment they begin to unfurl in spring to the point where they wither gracefully in autumn, ferns ooze style and beauty. If you can offer them a cool, shady spot and keep the plants well watered, they will reward you with a long-lasting, sophisticated display of rich greenery.

All ferns will grow in containers, although they resent being allowed to dry out. Tender tropical ferns are grown as houseplants, adoring the humidity of bathrooms and kitchens, but most ferns are very hardy and easy to grow in continually moist soil. With one or two exceptions, they prefer neutral to alkaline soil, so pot them into ordinary potting mix. They look at home in hollowed-out logs and other natural-looking containers.

Many ferns die down after the first frost, but some dryopteris retain their bronzed fronds well into winter. Others, such as the hart's tongue fern (*Asplenium scolopendrium*), are evergreen. As a precaution, leave the old fronds in position to protect the crown in winter, but cut them away as soon as replacement ones begin to emerge.

There are numerous types of ferns and many variants. Athyriums are deciduous and include the 4-foot-tall lady fern (*A. filix-femina*) and the much shorter but wide-spreading Japanese painted fern (*A. niponicum* var. *pictum*), which has silver fronds. The shuttlecock fern (*Matteuccia struthiopteris*, pictured above) is well named and makes a bold statement.

Beside the sea: 1

One of the most rewarding aspects of growing plants in containers is the opportunity to create evocative micro-themes, capable of transporting you from your own garden to another land entirely. A sunny seaside corner is especially effective and can be incorporated easily into just about any garden. The sea-green glaze of the main pot lends a maritime feel and architectural evergreens, including a phormium and yuccas, pick up the seaside theme.

The main focus here is the spiky foliage of clump-forming *Yucca filamentosa* 'Bright Edge', which carries a band of bright yellow along the edges of each sword-like

leaf. In contrast, the blue-green leaves of *Euphorbia myrsinites* clothe long, prostrate stems that dangle loosely over the edge of the pot. A mulch of small pebbles will hide any exposed soil and emphasize the architectural qualities of the yuccas. For detail, tiny pots of succulents sit among the pebbles.

You cannot really have too many pots in this arrangement, so an assortment of small terracotta pots has been stuffed with drought-tolerant houseleeks (*Sempervivum*) and stonecrops (*Sedum*) and placed in front of the main pot. To one side, the stiff, upright bronze-red leaves of *Phormium* 'Bronze Baby', a dwarf evergreen reaching 2 feet in height, make a pleasing contrast.

Finally, a 'beach' of cobbles, strewn with driftwood, coiled rope, seashells and other nautical *objets d'art*, supplies an air of authenticity.

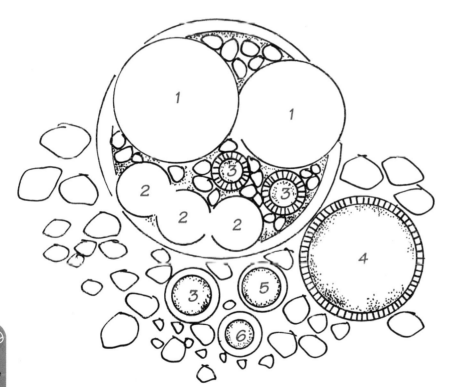

planting key

1 *Yucca filamentosa* 'Bright Edge'
2 *Euphorbia myrsinites*
3 *Sempervivum arachnoideum*
4 *Phormium* 'Bronze Baby'
5 *Sedum acre* 'Aureum'
6 *Sedum humifusum*

plant close-up

PHORMIUMS

Comfortable in full sun or considerable shade, phormiums, or New Zealand flax, are perfect sculptural evergreens and the best-behaved and most hardworking of container plants.

The two main species, *P. cookianum* and *P. tenax*, both grow too large for the average pot, but they have given rise to dwarf cultivars that grow between 30 inches and 4 feet high. Some are distinctly lax in habit with arching, strap-like leaves, while others are more rigidly upright, their leaves just drooping at the tips. Among the best of the former is *P. cookianum* subsp. *hookeri* 'Cream Delight', guaranteed to brighten a dull corner with its broadly cream-striped leaves. *P.* 'Evening Glow' has a similar habit, but comes in shades of pinky red and looks stunning in a blue pot. *P.* 'Jester' is upright with deep pink leaves edged in bright green, while the strawberry-pink leaves of *P.* 'Pink Panther' (pictured above) have burgundy borders.

In many places, phormiums are hardy enough to survive the winter outdoors even in pots. However, moving them to a more protected place is worthwhile because they rot quickly if they are too wet or if the roots freeze. Phormiums gradually spread sideways, forming strong clumps that can be divided carefully in spring or early summer.

Beside the sea: 2

People with coastal gardens are faced with many problems that inland gardeners do not have to consider. The most obvious of these is salt-laden wind, and the solution involves creating a tough, wind-filtering screen behind which your most precious and more vulnerable plants can grow.

These pots accommodate shrubs that are well equipped to cope with coastal conditions in the shelter of a windbreak. The pots, in varying sizes to suit each shrub, are glazed or painted in shades of aqua, turquoise and green, echoing the seaside theme. All but the fuchsia are evergreen and are chosen for their contrasting foliage.

Largest of the group, *Choisya* 'Aztec Pearl' can be pruned carefully after flowering to keep it compact.

Besides bearing clusters of scented white flowers in spring and early summer, it develops into a mound of deep green, finely fingered foliage and makes the perfect backdrop to the other shrubs in this group. Immediately in front, *Brachyglottis monroi* spreads wide and low and is clothed in grayish, olive-green leaves, attractively crinkled at their edges. It, too, can be trimmed to keep it neat. In summer, bright yellow, daisy-like flowers appear. Tucked in to the right is *Hebe rakaiensis*, a dense mound of tiny oval leaves studded in summer with pure white flowers. A pool of glossy dark purple is contributed by *Pittosporum tenuifolium* 'Tom Thumb', a bun-shaped dwarf shrub with bright green new leaves that color gradually as they age.

The red-and-purple flowers of *Fuchsia* 'Tom Thumb' dance in the gentlest breeze and are produced all summer long.

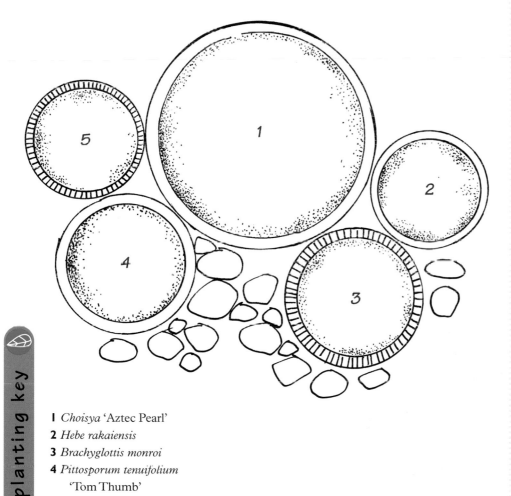

planting key

1 *Choisya* 'Aztec Pearl'
2 *Hebe rakaiensis*
3 *Brachyglottis monroi*
4 *Pittosporum tenuifolium* 'Tom Thumb'
5 *Fuchsia* 'Tom Thumb'

plant close-up

COASTAL-GARDEN PLANTS

Most coastal gardens take a battering from salt-laden winds that can decimate many plants, burning their leaves and causing more permanent damage. However, some plants cope with having salt deposited on their leaves if they are offered shelter from the wind.

First, erect a windbreak of fine mesh or create an evergreen screen of salt- and wind-tolerant shrubs such as elaeagnus or griselinia. That done, there are a surprising number of shrubs, conifers and perennials that will thrive in coastal gardens, whether in pots or in the open ground.

Among their number are a fair proportion of evergreens. These include the strawberry tree (*Arbutus unedo*, pictured above), although in due course it will outgrow even the largest pot, Mexican orange blossom (*Choisya ternata*), hebes, daisy bushes (*Olearia*), tree heathers (*Erica arborea*) and escallonias. Cabbage palms (*Cordyline*), grown for their spiky architectural appearance, and many low-growing evergreens including lavenders (*Lavandula*), junipers (*Juniperus*) and dwarf pines (*Pinus*), should also thrive. In frost-prone areas, insulate the pots in winter with polyethylene bubble wrap, foam or old blankets and drape row cover material over the foliage.

Of the deciduous shrubs that flourish by the sea, red-and-purple-flowered *Fuchsia magellanica*, feathery pink tamarisk (*Tamarix*) and hydrangeas should all succeed in large pots.

Good enough to eat

In many gardens it just isn't practical to have a dedicated vegetable patch, perhaps because the soil is too shallow or because time or space simply do not allow. However, a number of vegetables can grow successfully in containers and provide fresh produce close at hand, without excessive effort. This collection of simple salad vegetables includes pole beans, lettuce and tomatoes.

'Hestia' is a dwarf pole bean growing only 18 inches tall, covered with masses of scarlet-and-white flowers that result in crops of stringless beans. Provide a little support and pick regularly to keep it cropping.

Dwarf varieties of tomato are also well suited to growing in containers. 'Totem' F1 is a bushy, upright variety that bears good-sized red fruit and sits happily with the pole beans.

Colored- and fancy-leaved lettuces are worth growing for their ornamental appeal but all are good in salads, too. They are an excellent, fast-maturing crop and we have used loose-leaved "picking" varieties that can be cut a few leaves at a time rather than harvested whole. The wine-red leaves of 'Red Salad Bowl' are set off to perfection against frilly, green 'Frillice'.

The dull, weathered gray of fiberglass or plastic containers designed to look like lead underline the lush leafiness of the vegetables, while *Ipomoea* 'Mini Sky Blue', a miniature-flowered morning glory, scrambles up spiral metal plant supports to add a little extra color.

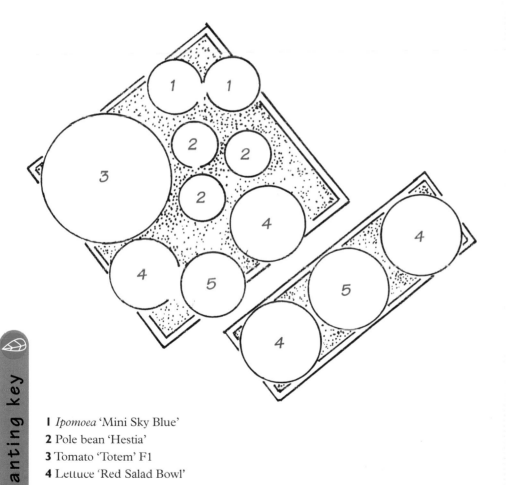

planting key

1 *Ipomoea* 'Mini Sky Blue'
2 Pole bean 'Hestia'
3 Tomato 'Totem' F1
4 Lettuce 'Red Salad Bowl'
5 Lettuce 'Frillice'

plant close-up

VEGETABLES

Even in the tiniest space it is possible to grow vegetables. Many new varieties are being bred both for dwarfness and for their ornamental appeal, so your containers won't be dull.

Fast-maturing produce such as lettuce, radish, beets and tiny carrots are the most suitable for containers. They can be started in flats or cells or sown directly into the container and thinned as necessary. Make successional sowings and you will be reaping the rewards for weeks. Peas and beans are also suitable, but choose dwarf varieties that do not require too much support. For a cottage garden feel, add herbs such as parsley and sage and a handful of scented flowers like sweet peas (*Lathyrus odoratus*) and pinks (*Dianthus*).

More demanding vegetables such as tomatoes and cucumbers need a great deal of attention, but with regular watering and fertilizing will crop well. Peppers, chillies (pictured above) and eggplants are also good candidates, but to get the best from any container-grown produce keep the soil moist. Position the pots in full sun to ensure that the fruits ripen, but keep the roots cool by standing them among groups of potted annuals. A mulch will help to conserve moisture. If you go up to a half-barrel size container you can even try growing potatoes and full-size pole beans.

Berry tasty

Many fruiting plants are suitable for container culture. You can cram all your edible plants into a few well-chosen, sizable pots and pick them when you need them from the comfort of a reclining chair, while relaxing on your patio and savoring the sweet aromas of blueberries, strawberries and others.

Even just a couple of pots of fruit are worthwhile and, with the exception of particularly vigorous kinds such as raspberries and blackberries, there is a good range to try. When laden, fruit bushes can be as attractive as many plants grown purely for their aesthetic appeal, although at other times they may be less attractive. The answer is to move them to a less prominent spot or hide them with a few pots of flowers.

Strawberries are one of the fruits most frequently grown in pots, partly because they have a head start over slugs and snails and partly because they take up less ground space when grown in plastic towers or terracotta strawberry pots. Here we've teamed up perpetual fruiting 'Aromel' with other edible berries including standard 'Industria' red currants and 'Invicta' gooseberries, each pruned to be on a short stem to lend

height. 'Bluecrop', which is a compact blueberry, adds a touch of the unusual.

For the best crops, choose a spot that does not heat up drastically but still receives plenty of sun and pots that are large and deep. They will also need copious amounts of water to ensure the fruits swell. A mulch of cocoa shells will help. A couple of smaller pots brimming with alpine strawberries round off this tasty gathering.

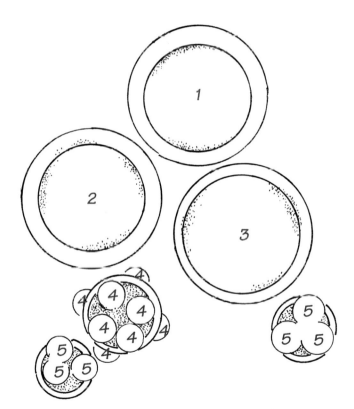

planting key

1 Red currant 'Industria'
2 Gooseberry 'Invicta'
3 Blueberry 'Bluecrop'
4 Strawberry 'Aromel'
5 Alpine strawberry 'Semperflorens'

plant close-up

BLUEBERRIES

Imagine stepping out onto the patio and picking enough blueberries to make your own pie. Once established, even a single container-grown blueberry will yield enough fruit to earn its keep.

Highbush blueberries bear clusters of dark purplish-blue fruits that are covered in a white bloom. The fruit ripens over several weeks during mid- to late summer and the flavor is enhanced by cooking or preserving. Besides bearing delicious, attractive fruit, blueberries have leaves that turn stunning shades of red and gold before they fall in autumn. Small white flowers appear in spring. Depending on variety, the bushes will grow 4–6 feet high. The shorter, more compact kinds are ideally suited to growing in large containers.

Although blueberries are self-fertile, a greater crop is assured if you plant two or more different cultivars in close proximity. They require an acid soil, so pot them up in ericaceous (lime-free) soil mix and keep it moist but not too wet. They will appreciate a sunny position, but not one that becomes scorchingly hot, and are also happy in light shade.

The berries are borne on two- to three-year-old wood, so initial cropping will be minimal. Young bushes require very little pruning – just remove weak shoots in order to form a strong framework. Prune to encourage new shoots from the base by completely removing some of the oldest branches each year.

Clambering clematis

One of the most reliable ways to gain height in containers, whether on the patio, flanking steps or guarding the front door, is to grow climbers over a specially constructed framework.

This trio of clematis grows on a pyramid of wooden trellis in a large, square wooden planter, and provides flowers in complementary shades throughout the second half of summer. Because all three are late-flowering, they can be cut back hard in spring. This allows the frame to be painted or renewed without disturbing the plants. We have used three clematis together to achieve an eye-catching color combination, but they will need a very large pot. If you find this is too ambitious, try a pair or just a single specimen instead.

The most vigorous of this threesome is pale, pearly-pink flowered C. 'Huldine'. Capable of reaching 12 feet or more, its stems should be carefully spiralled and woven through the frame as it grows. Brighter and more unusual, C. 'Gravetye Beauty' bears elegantly poised, upward-facing, tulip-shaped blooms in a rich shade of scarlet-red. At 4 inches across, the mauve-pink flowers of C. 'Victoria' are the largest of the three. As an alternative, consider combining lavender-blue C. 'Arabella', light blue C. 'Prince Charles' and rich purple C. 'Polish Spirit'.

If possible, ensure that the pot itself is shaded by other plants in order to keep the roots of the clematis cool. Don't forget to water copiously and fertilize twice a month. Tie in the brittle new shoots as they appear to prevent them from snapping off.

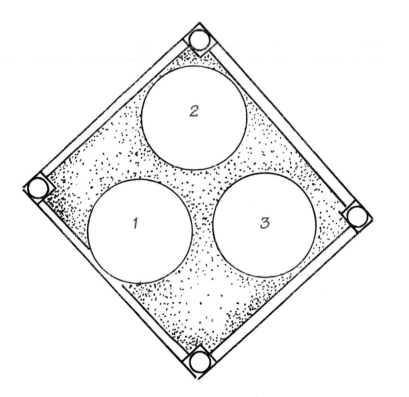

1 *Clematis* 'Huldine'
2 *Clematis* 'Gravetye Beauty'
3 *Clematis* 'Victoria'

plant close-up

CLIMBERS

Most climbers are too vigorous for containers, because they have a massive root system to support the tangle of top growth. However, the less rampant kinds can be grown successfully provided you lavish them with care.

First, choose the largest container you can: it should be at least 2 feet deep and wide. The smaller the pot, the sooner the plants will outgrow it and the more difficult they will be to care for. They will also need some form of support. If the plants are to grow against a wall or a fence, use horizontal wires or trellis made of wood or plastic. If they are destined to be free-standing, they will require a framework.

Whatever basic framework you choose, it should be in keeping with the style of both the pot and your house. The simplest structures can be made from bamboo canes or even lengthy prunings from buddleias or other shrubs with tall, straight stems. Push the canes in around the edge of the pot to form a pyramid and tie them together at the top. The least expensive ready-made frames are those constructed from willow, although they have a limited life. Timber, metal and plastic-coated frames are also available in a variety of styles.

Try less vigorous clematis, jasmine (*Jasminum*), ivies (*Hedera*), honeysuckles (*Lonicera*) and climbing herbaceous plants, like yellow-flowered *Dicentra macrocapnos* and blue *Clematis* x *durandii* (pictured above).

Rosy view

Whether on a patio, in the center of a gravel bed planted with scented lavender or greeting you at the gate, even the smallest garden can afford space for at least one or two roses. This collection is a spin-off from the grouping on pages 60–61, using patio climbing roses in place of clematis.

Here we have kept the same wooden planters as before, but replaced the frame with a taller, more slender obelisk made from plastic-coated tubular steel. Rose stems are not as easy to weave in and out as those of clematis, so it is important to choose a support that will take their full height of around 6 feet. The container, and even the obelisk itself, can be painted to complement the color of the flowers.

Rosa 'Laura Ford' is an excellent climbing patio rose that opens its strong yellow flowers early in the season and continues through the summer. In hot weather the blooms have a pinkish tinge and in autumn they develop an amber glow. The climbing stems are densely clothed from head to toe with healthy, dark green foliage. Orange-vermilion *R.* 'Warm Welcome' combines beautifully with *R.* 'Laura Ford', creating a cheery, almost luminous pairing. At the base of the roses, cream-and-blue *Viola* 'Magnifico' F1 will quickly cover any bare soil and, if deadheaded regularly, will bloom all through summer and autumn.

In a smaller container, *R.* 'Sweet Dream', a dwarf cluster-flowered bush rose, picks up the color theme with its peachy-apricot flowers producing flush after flush throughout summer.

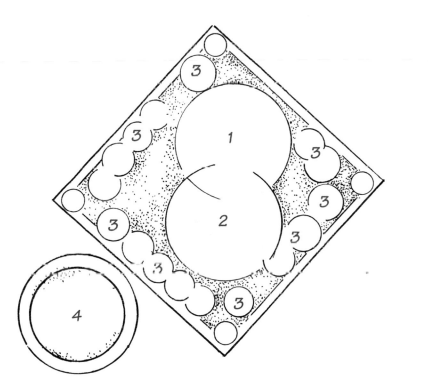

planting key

1 *Rosa* 'Laura Ford'
2 *Rosa* 'Warm Welcome'
3 *Viola* 'Magnifico' F1
4 *Rosa* 'Sweet Dream'

plant close-up

ROSES FOR CONTAINERS

Roses are widely planted and one of the breakthroughs of recent years is the 'patio' or dwarf cluster-flowered bush rose.

Patio roses have a compact, bushy habit and grow an average of just 20 inches tall, so are perfect for containers. Their flowers are borne in dense clusters over a long period during summer and autumn and some are sweetly scented.

R. 'Gentle Touch' (pictured above) is pale pink with dainty, well-formed flowers carried in clusters on sturdy plants. In contrast, the fragrant blooms of *R.* 'Sweet Memories' are lemon-yellow and of medium size. Bearing salmon-pink blooms, *R.* 'Tip Top' has a fragrance reminiscent of wild roses and is very disease resistant. *R.* 'Top Marks' is neat and sturdy, and deserving of its name with its vermilion flowers and disease resistance.

Roses dislike light soils. In containers plant them in a loam-based mix, with the knob where they were budded onto their rootstock sitting 1 inch below the surface. If you are planting patio roses in a large pot, space them about 12 inches apart.

To encourage continual flowering, remove individual blooms as they wither and cut faded clusters back to an emerging shoot. Be vigilant about aphids and spray accordingly. Prune patio bush roses in autumn or spring, cutting back the main stems to an outward-facing bud (12–16 inches) above ground level and reducing sideshoots by one-third of their length.

A taste of the Orient

The meditative tranquillity of a Japanese garden is surprisingly easy to emulate using a variety of foliage plants in containers. Dwarf bamboos, Japanese maples (*Acer palmatum* and *A. japonicum*), carefully chosen pots and oriental accessories can all be called upon to generate an authentic, soothing atmosphere.

The background here is dominated by the mushroom-like form of *Acer palmatum* var. *dissectum* 'Inaba-shidare', a cut-leaved Japanese maple clad with neatly fingered, deep burgundy-red leaves, planted in a large, curved-sided pot. The plant's gently weeping habit is echoed by a mound of *Hakonechloa macra* 'Aureola', its soft, tactile, yellow-and-green striped leaves flowing calmly over the edge. The leaves of this deciduous

perennial grass from Japan are brightest when sited in light shade. The Japanese maple is also best kept out of the full glare of the sun to protect its leaves from scorching.

Sometimes decorated with oriental-style motifs, heavy-duty glazed pots really evoke the mood of the Far East. Here a grouping of different sized pots contains *Fargesia murielae* 'Simba', a short, compact, clump-forming bamboo loosely attired in bright green leaves, and a dwarf, pinkish-purple Japanese azalea, *Rhododendron* 'Hatsugiri'. The effect of the bamboo is bulked up with a few chunky lengths of cane pushed in among its slender stems.

At ground level, a pair of granite candle holders sits on a bed of gravel laid in a shallow bowl. A few well-placed boulders could easily complete this stress-relieving scene.

JAPANESE MAPLES

Japanese maples (*Acer palmatum* and *A. japonicum*) lend a touch of class to containers. Often considered difficult to grow, they are actually very easy, given the right conditions.

They dislike cold winds, especially in spring when the young foliage is unfurling. Hot sun can also have a scorching effect, so site them in a sheltered, lightly shaded spot. Use a fibrous potting mixture (ericaceous, or lime-free, mix is fine, but not essential) and keep it evenly moist, but not wet, especially in summer.

Most Japanese maples will eventually form small trees although some make large shrubs, wider than they are high. Spring and summer foliage varies from light green through pale yellow to wine-red, while the autumn tints range from yellow through glowing orange to red.

Among the best are *A. palmatum* 'Garnet', a cut-leaved, burgundy-red variety that forms a mound of cascading branches, and *A. shirasawanum* 'Aureum', which is very slow-growing with fan-like leaves of golden yellow, fading to lime-green. A faster-growing kind is *A. palmatum* 'Atropurpureum' (pictured above), while for autumn color choose *A. p.* 'Osakazuki', a fiery-hued, upright variety.

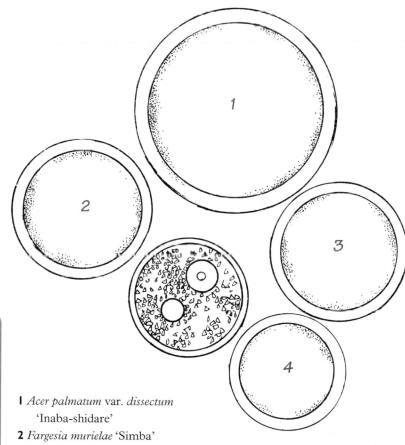

planting key

1 *Acer palmatum* var. *dissectum* 'Inaba-shidare'
2 *Fargesia murielae* 'Simba'
3 *Hakonechloa macra* 'Aureola'
4 *Rhododendron* 'Hatsugiri'

Mexican fever

In contrast to the tranquil oriental pots on pages 64–65, this busy grouping is packed with summer color for a sizzling display, evocative of the heat and vibrancy of Mexico and Brazil.

A large, curvaceous oval pot houses the main planting that is presided over by dwarf, multi-headed sunflowers (*Helianthus annuus* 'Dwarf Yellow Spray') whose cheery bright yellow blooms are produced freely throughout the summer. In the middle are dahlias and daisy-flowered rudbeckias in complementary fiery shades. *Rudbeckia hirta* 'Toto' is one of a number of annual varieties that are easily grown from seed and with regular deadheading, it will bloom for months. Dwarf dahlias are also invaluable for containers due to their sheer

variety – the Gallery Series, including bright orange *D.* 'Gallery Art Deco', are particularly compact and floriferous. As a contrast, *Stipa tenuissima*, a silky, slender-stemmed grass, erupts from among the dahlias.

Stiffly branching *Lantana camara*, in a shade of burnt orange-red, spreads over the edge of the main pot, while *Petunia* 'Million Bells Lemon' tumbles down the side and, with a little encouragement, will also scramble up through the other plants. A word of warning here: lantana is a skin irritant, so treat it with respect.

To finish off the display, the two smaller pots at the front contain a repeat of *Dahlia* 'Gallery Art Deco' and a fancy-leaved coleus (*Solenostemon* 'Wizard Scarlet') underplanted with luminous *Dorotheanthus bellidiformis* mixed, which open their colorful daisy blooms wide in full sun.

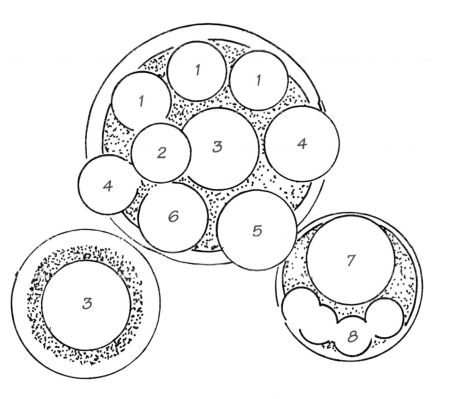

planting key

1 *Helianthus annuus* 'Dwarf Yellow Spray'
2 *Stipa tenuissima*
3 *Dahlia* 'Gallery Art Deco'
4 *Rudbeckia hirta* 'Toto'

5 *Petunia* 'Million Bells Lemon'
6 *Lantana camara*
7 *Solenostemon* 'Wizard Scarlet'
8 *Dorotheanthus bellidiformis* mixed

plant close-up

DAHLIAS

Native to Mexico and Central America, dahlias are hard to beat for providing a splash of color for a warm, sunny spot. The range of shades – from blazing oranges and reds through subtler pinks and mauves to white – allows them to fit into any color scheme, and the dwarf kinds are perfectly suited to growing in containers.

Flowers are very showy, varying in form from tight pompons to spiky 'cactuses'. Good seed mixtures include *D.* 'Diablo' and *D.* 'Redskin' – both have dark, bronze-red leaves that are an excellent foil for the bright flowers. These are annuals, best discarded at the end of the season. Also grown from seed, but worth keeping from year to year, is *D.* 'Bishop's Children', a mixture derived from dark-leaved, scarlet-flowered *D.* 'Bishop of Llandaff' (pictured above) and its kin.

Individually named dahlia varieties can be obtained as tubers or rooted cuttings. Start tubers in gentle warmth during early spring and detach some of the young shoots to make new plants, or cut large tubers into smaller sections. Pot them up and place outdoors once all danger of frost has passed. In containers, they are less easily targeted by slugs and snails.

Among the best dwarfs are deep-red, cactus-flowered *D.* 'Red Pygmy', yellow-and-orange striped *D.* 'Washington', and the Gallery Series including yellow *D.* 'Gallery Cezanne', lilac-tinged white *D.* 'Gallery Art Fair' and pink *D.* 'Gallery Salvador'.

Autumn glow

In autumn, flowers take a back seat and make way for the warm glow of leaves and fruits in fiery shades of orange, red, gold and yellow. The spirit of autumn can be captured very successfully in a container by using shrubs that bear berries and choosing evergreens that have colored leaves.

Set in a large terracotta pot, the backbone of this planting is orange-berried *Pyracantha* 'Teton', a reliable, semi-evergreen shrub that can be pruned into many shapes. *Ilex crenata* 'Golden Gem', an equally hardy dwarf holly, has complementary golden-yellow leaves that densely cover low, spreading branches. To complete the main pot, *Hedera helix* 'Adam' dangles over the edge, its trailing stems furnished with creamy-white-and-

yellow variegated leaves. In a sunny or very lightly shaded spot, this eye-catching combination will last well into winter.

Dark blue winter pansies (*Viola × wittrockiana* Ultima Series) greet the eye in the foreground, working well with the oranges and yellows in the main pot. *Gaultheria procumbens*, a dwarf, spreading evergreen with long-lasting, aromatic red berries, sits in the middle; it

needs ericaceous (lime-free) soil.

The pansies may stop flowering during very hot weather; grow them in their own individual pot. In this way, they are easily removed while not in flower and returned once they begin blooming again.

To spice things up temporarily, add a few props. Here, a handful of brightly colored, different-shaped gourds have been arranged on a bed of straw in an unplanted terracotta pot.

HOLLIES

Hollies (*Ilex*) are among the most noble of evergreens; their stature, glossy leaves and bright red berries (those of *I × altaclarensis* are pictured above) contribute to their appeal. Their slow growth and resilience make hollies easy to grow in large pots where they eventually form imposing specimens. Responsive to clipping and pruning, they are also popular as topiary plants.

Besides the green-leaved hollies, there are a number with varying degrees of leaf variegation and a few with distinctly blue-tinged foliage. Berry color can also vary and, although most are red, a few are orange, yellow or even black.

In most cases, a male and a female plant must grow near each other in order for berries — borne by the female — to appear. However, *I. aquifolium* 'J.C. van Tol' and *I. a.* 'Pyramidalis', among others, are both self-fertile. Confusingly, *I. × altaclarensis* 'Golden King' is female and *I. aquifolium* 'Silver Queen' is male. For the brightest variegation grow *I. a.* 'Golden Milkboy' and for the prickliest leaves choose *I. a.* 'Ferox Argentea'. Among the best of the blue hollies is *I. meservae* 'Blue Girl', a free-fruiting female. Dwarf hollies such as *I. crenata* 'Golden Gem' have tiny, spineless leaves and are well worth growing, although their black berries are not significant.

Hollies will grow in either sun or shade, and although not fussy about soil conditions they prefer to be kept reasonably moist. Overgrown plants can be cut back severely in early summer.

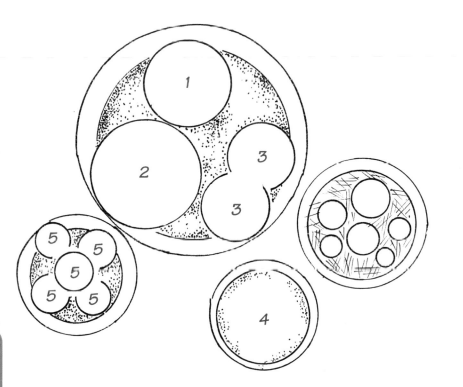

1 *Pyracantha* 'Teton'
2 *Ilex crenata* 'Golden Gem'
3 *Hedera helix* 'Adam'
4 *Gaultheria procumbens*
5 *Viola × wittrockiana* Ultima Series (blue shades)

Troughs and window boxes

Troughs and window boxes offer the opportunity of cramming plants into small, restricted spaces such as windowsills where most other containers simply would not fit. Because they are rectangular and often narrow, you can push them together to make more economic use of space, and they are particularly useful for patio areas or roof gardens.

For anyone who enjoys growing a wide variety of plants, windowsills without window boxes are an opportunity missed. They offer the chance to site herbs and salad vegetables close at hand and scented plants where you can enjoy them both indoors and out.

Window boxes can also be attached to structures such as railings, and many a dull wall can be brightened instantly by fixing up a few flower-filled troughs. Secured to a wall in troughs, tiny alpine plants can be brought nearer to eye level where their exquisite detail can be readily admired, while trailing plants will reach their full potential dangling from high up on a wall or ledge.

Used at ground level, troughs can be planted with tall sunflowers or annual climbing plants supported on a simple wire framework to achieve effective temporary screening. By fixing ornamental boxes permanently to the wall or sill and placing easily removed plastic troughs inside, you can change a tired display in an instant, especially if you have a replacement waiting in the wings.

Window boxes can also be made to measure, ensuring that not even the tiniest bit of space is wasted and that the style of the box and the material from which it is made is in keeping with its setting. Wooden, lattice-patterned boxes suit period homes, for instance, while reflective stainless steel echoes the crisp minimalist feel of many contemporary dwellings.

Winter wonderland

In winter, window boxes really come into their own and allow you to squeeze lots of seasonal color into a very small space – preferably close to the house where it can be most appreciated. This busy, symmetrical gathering of plants for autumn, winter and spring is guaranteed to delight.

At the center of the action is a dwarf spruce, *Picea glauca* var. *albertiana* 'Conica', with dark-green needles clothing its conical form from top to bottom. Heathers always associate well with conifers and *Erica arborea* 'Albert's Gold', a tall-growing, golden-yellow tree heather, is no exception. Tree heathers need an acid soil and although none of the other plants here is particularly demanding of acidic conditions, they will all thrive in the same ericaceous (lime-free) mix that suits the heathers.

The blooms of bright red *Cyclamen* 'Miracle' offer a cheery contribution, and the dull gray of the lead look-alike fiberglass trough emphasizes their showiness. Although it is not completely frost hardy, the cyclamen will survive well into the winter – and usually beyond – if given shelter and not overwatered. Bred for use in autumn and winter containers, they can also be used in cool, bright indoor rooms.

Two winter-flowering heaths, *Erica × darleyensis* 'Silberschmelze' and *E. carnea* 'December Red', are crowded with white or deep pinkish-red blooms respectively from midwinter onward and serve to fill out the foreground. Finally, in a late-winter flourish, *Iris* 'Joyce', a dwarf reticulata variety, pops up its pretty heads in a rich shade of blue.

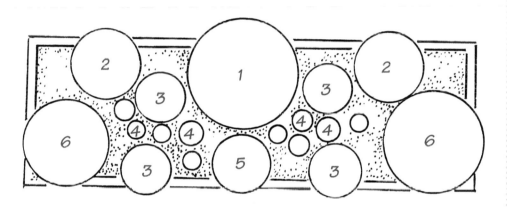

planting key

1 *Picea glauca* var. *albertiana* 'Conica'
2 *Erica arborea* 'Albert's Gold'
3 *Cyclamen* 'Miracle'
4 *Iris* 'Joyce'
5 *Erica carnea* 'December Red'
6 *Erica × darleyensis* 'Silberschmelze'

plant close-up

DWARF CONIFERS

Truly dwarf conifers are ideal subjects for containers, especially when combined with heathers (*Erica* and *Calluna*) or alpine plants. They are mostly well behaved, and with sufficient care will last for many years.

Even though they are slow-growing, dwarf conifers are far from boring. Their foliage changes with the seasons and the new growth of some is as bright as any flower. *Chamaecyparis pisifera* 'Plumosa Aurea', for example, enters spring ablaze with feathery golden-yellow new shoots. *Cryptomeria japonica* 'Compressa', on the other hand, is deep green in summer but in late autumn turns reddish bronze.

Dwarf conifers have very reliable leaf coloring but vary considerably in shape and habit. Some, like *Juniperus communis* 'Compressa', are pencil thin, while others are conical. Many others develop into mounds, like the dwarf spruce *Picea mariana* 'Nana' or *Thuja occidentalis* 'Danica'. *Picea pungens* 'Globosa', a distinct form of blue spruce, becomes a prickly dome of steely blue, while dwarf cultivars of *Pinus mugo* (pictured above), the tiniest of all pines, build into loose blue, green or gold needle-clad hummocks.

Among the junipers are ground-hugging varieties such as *Juniperus sabina* 'Tamariscifolia' and *J. procumbens* 'Nana'. They make good surface cover, softening the edges of containers, and a little pruning easily keeps them in order.

All lined up

Some plants bear flowers that are too unmanageable for their own good, and that is certainly true of *Narcissus* 'Rip van Winkle'. Its bright yellow starry blooms consist of so many petals that their slender stems bend under the weight. In the garden they usually end up lying battered on the soil, but lined up in a trough they will nod gently over the sides, without any danger of the flowers becoming damaged.

A traditional terracotta trough with a simple fluted pattern is the setting for these harbingers of spring; its warm tones echo their sunny faces. As a backdrop, the slender, bronze-brown curls of *Carex comans* are hard to

beat. Dangling like a fringe over the heads of the narcissi, this hardy sedge is evergreen and on a sheltered, sunny windowsill will keep its coloring throughout the winter.

Pushing up in front, densely planted glory-of-the-snow (*Chionodoxa luciliae*) forms a carpet of china-blue, white-centered stars. Growing a little taller, *Puschkinia scilloides* sends up 6-inch-tall spikes of palest silver-blue. As a darker

blue alternative to either, try *Scilla siberica* or blue *Anemone blanda*. A surface mulch of bark chips, moss or leafmold is a final embellishment.

The carex will look good long after the bulbs have faded and can be split and replanted in the trough before being joined in summer by yellow, daisy-flowered *Bidens ferulifolia* and, in the front line, *Convolvulus sabatius*, a trailing plant bearing small, silver-blue blooms.

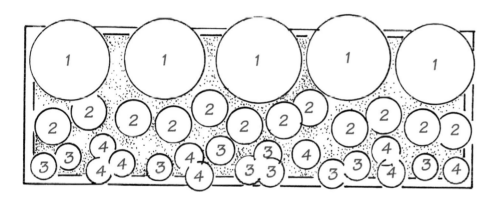

planting key

1 *Carex comans* bronze
2 *Narcissus* 'Rip van Winkle'
3 *Puschkinia scilloides*
4 *Chionodoxa luciliae*

plant close-up

EVERGREEN GRASSES

Cultivated for their varied foliage and forms, ornamental grasses provide a foil to flowering plants and look equally good planted together or with other foliage plants such as heucheras, tiarellas and hostas. There is a huge range of grasses available, mostly thanks to their all-year-round displays of texture and form, and their ease of cultivation.

Included under the same banner are the sedges: although similar in appearance, they generally thrive in damper soils than grasses and some can be grown in shallow water. Of the many evergreens, *Carex*, a varied genus of colorful sedges, is perhaps the largest group. As evergreen foliage plants for containers, these are hard to beat. *C. morrowii* 'Fisher' is reminiscent of an indoor spider plant (*Chlorophytum*), but is completely hardy and ideal for year-round displays. *C. oshimensis* 'Evergold' (pictured above) lives up to its name, while *C. comans* 'Frosted Curls' forms tight clumps of silvery, mint-green leaves that spill over the edges of containers. *C. flagellifera* is similar to the bronze *C. comans* in the terracotta trough opposite, but is larger and broader-growing.

Acorus gramineus 'Ogon', another moisture-lover, exhibits yellow-edged leaves in fan-like clusters. Less reliably evergreen, blue fescue (*Festuca glauca*) has a tidier appearance when sheltered from the worst of the winter and not allowed to dry out.

Mountain scene

When you are restricted for space, or if you simply want to cram in the maximum number of plants, tiny gem-like alpines or rock plants are undoubtedly the answer in a sunny spot.

The traditional containers for alpines are sinks carved from stone, but these are now difficult and expensive to obtain. However, substitutes made from concrete or lightweight materials are readily available.

Adding height and scale here is *Juniperus communis* 'Compressa', a slim, upright dwarf conifer. Two carefully placed lumps of tufa (a porous, lightweight limestone into which plants can be inserted) provide structure. A covering of grit helps the drainage around each plant, and grit is also mixed into the soil mix.

It is important to choose plants that are matched in vigor in order to prevent the tiniest ones from being quickly swamped. Among the most petite are some of the saxifrages. Here, a tight, silvery-green hummock of *Saxifraga* 'Jenkinsiae' is studded with pink flowers, while *S.* 'Gregor Mendel' bears yellow blooms. Trailing over the edge are soft pink *Phlox douglasii* 'Boothman's Variety' and deep pink *P. d.* 'Crackerjack'. *Raoulia*

hookeri forms a pool of silver leaves beneath the juniper.

To extend flowering well into summer, we have added fleshy-leaved *Lewisia cotyledon* hybrids, available in a range of colors, and a drift of pink *Rhodohypoxis baurii*. They both enjoy lime-free soil and are planted in pots of ericaceous soil mix and "plunged." Finally, more lumps of tufa rock on the ground are a home for houseleeks (*Sempervivum*).

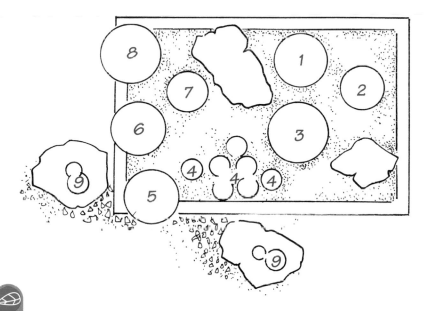

planting key

1 *Juniperus communis* 'Compressa'
2 *Saxifraga* 'Jenkinsiae'
3 *Raoulia hookeri*
4 *Rhodohypoxis baurii* mixed
5 *Phlox douglasii* 'Crackerjack'
6 *Lewisia cotyledon* hybrids
7 *Saxifraga* 'Gregor Mendel'
8 *Phlox douglasii* 'Boothman's Variety'
9 *Sempervivum* 'Red Mountain'

plant close-up

RHODOHYPOXIS

Rhodohypoxis are gem-like miniatures that grow wild in the mountain meadows of South Africa where summer rainfall is heavy, but in winter they are covered by a blanket of snow.

They are tiny enough to be squeezed into any garden, and will obligingly fill any small container with grassy leaves and a carpet of starry flowers. The blooms are composed of six flat petals and carried on 2–4-inch stems that appear in profusion from spring until early autumn. Their colors range from a deepest pink that is almost red through sugary pale pinks to white.

R. baurii is the most common species and has given rise to several excellent cultivars, including deep pink *R.* 'Albrighton' (pictured above) and pure white, large-flowered *R.* 'Helen'. *R.* 'Margaret Rose' is pale pink, while the magenta-pink blooms of *R.* 'Harlequin' are flushed with white. Vigorous *R. milloides* tolerates more moisture and produces cerise-pink flowers.

Although frost hardy, *Rhodohypoxis* detest being wet while dormant, and grow best in pots that can be moved into a greenhouse in winter. Here they can be kept almost completely dry before watering recommences in early spring. If you are growing them in alpine sinks that are too heavy and awkward to move, cover the container with a miniature cloche or a piece of glass.

Rhodohypoxis thrive in full sun and acidic soil. Pot up in a mixture of ericaceous soil mix and lime-free grit. Divide clumps in early spring.

Windowsill herbs

The handiest place to grow herbs for the kitchen is on a sunny windowsill or just outside the back door – and it is possible to grow most within the confines of a window box.

The herbs in this wooden window box include parsley, chives, basil, mint and thyme. Each plant is "plunged" into the box in a separate pot, so that it can be replaced easily when overgrown, and rampant types such as mint can be controlled. Use the largest pots you can, so that the plants have as long a life as possible before they need repotting. To ensure the good drainage most herbs prefer, fill the bottom of the window box and pots with a layer of coarse gravel or broken crocks.

Represented here in its curly form, *Mentha spicata* var. *crispa*, mint is surely an essential part of any culinary herb collection. Another must-have herb is basil, and in this case we have chosen to use the purple form *Ocimum basilicum* var. *purpurascens* for its decorative leaves that are especially good in rice dishes. Coriander (*Coriandrum sativum*) is also useful in a variety of recipes: harvest young leaves and add them to salads,

stews and curries, or use as a garnish. You can prolong the plants' lives in a pot by picking off mature leaves.

Parsley (*Petroselinum crispum*) and chives (*Allium schoenoprasum*) are also included; both of them need more water than the other herbs in this selection. At the front a creeping thyme, *Thymus serpyllum* 'Russetings', forms carpets of dark green leaves, dotted in summer with mauve-purple flowers.

plant close-up

BASILS

Despite their reputation as temperamental plants, many basils (*Ocimum*) are worth growing for their ornamental appeal as well as for their culinary use. Growing the plants in pots will allow you to regulate their watering and general care, thereby increasing your chances of success.

Basils are frost tender and grow best in warm positions where they are sheltered from cold winds. In frost-prone areas they must be treated as annuals, grown from seed and placed outdoors when all danger of frost has passed. Sow the seeds in individual pots or cell-trays to avoid root disturbance, which they resent. Ideally, water at midday or, if this is not possible, earlier rather than later. Basils hate to be overwatered.

Pinch out the tips of young plants to promote bushy growth and new leaves and to prevent flowering. When harvesting, select young leaves from the upper part of the plant. Basils repel flying insects and make good companions to plants such as tomatoes that are prone to attack.

Sweet basil (*O. basilicum*) is widely grown and its leaves are excellent in pasta sauces. By comparison, the leaves of bush basil (*O. minimum*) are tiny and look pretty in salads. It is one of the best varieties for small containers. *O. basilicum* 'Green Ruffles' (pictured above) bears large, crinkled, aniseed-flavored leaves that are bright green, while those of *O. b.* 'Purple Ruffles' are deep purple-red. Choose *O.* x *citriodorum* if you are looking for basil scent with a lemon flavor.

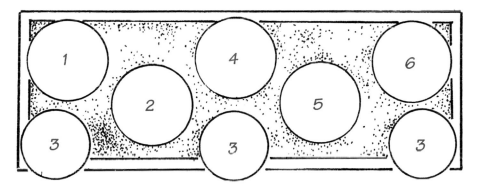

planting key

1 Coriander (*Coriandrum sativum*)
2 Chives (*Allium schoenoprasum*)
3 Creeping thyme (*Thymus serpyllum* 'Russetings')
4 Curly mint (*Mentha spicata* var. *crispa*)
5 Purple basil (*Ocimum basilicum* var. *purpurascens*)
6 Parsley (*Petroselinum crispum*)

Thyme time

The variation in habit, leaf and flower within one plant genus can be astounding. Thymes (*Thymus*) are a prime example, and as an alternative to the mixture of herbs on pages 78–79, we have dedicated the same wooden window box exclusively to various species and cultivars of thyme.

Forming the 12-inch-high back row are orange-scented thyme (*T.* 'Fragrantissimus'), with grayish-green leaves that are useful in stir-fry and poultry dishes, and lemon thyme (*T.* × *citriodorus*), which has relatively large lemon-scented green leaves that are superb in chicken or fish dishes. *T.* 'Porlock' also stands at the back, its bushy form clothed with mild-flavored leaves and pink summer flowers. It also has antibacterial qualities.

Filling in the middle ground are two of the most popular thymes, prized equally for their ornamental and culinary appeal. *T. vulgaris* 'Silver Posie' bears small silver-gray variegated leaves that are often tinged pink, while golden thyme (*T. pulegioides* 'Aureus') boasts leaves that are bright golden yellow through spring and summer. Both look good in salads.

Spilling over the front edge and grown purely for their ornamental merits are *T. pseudolanuginosus*, a gray-leaved, woolly thyme and two other prostrate thymes, *T.* 'Snowdrift' and *T. serpyllum* 'Pink Chintz'.

Other herbs that offer enough variation to be grown in single-genus groups like this include mint (*Mentha*), basil (*Ocimum*) and marjoram (*Origanum*). The same principle can be applied to many other plants from saxifrages (*Saxifraga*) to pelargoniums.

THYMES

A multi-talented group of plants, thymes (*Thymus*) are excellent for containers, because they have attractive flowers and leaves as well as culinary and medicinal uses. Some varieties are upright and bushy, while others are ideal for trailing over the edge of a pot.

All thymes relish full sun and a poor, well-drained soil; the most reliable way to grow them is in containers filled with a gritty, free-draining mix. Cut back plants after flowering to maintain a neat, compact habit.

Thymes are evergreen and there is a huge variety of leaf colors, ranging from the woolly gray of *T. pseudolanuginosus* to the bright gold of *T. x citriodorus* 'Archer's Gold'. All thyme leaves are aromatic: some are lemon-scented, while others are reminiscent of orange, camphor, celery and more. Thyme flowers appear in summer, and are usually pink or white. (*Thymus vulgaris* is pictured above.)

Of the carpeting kinds, *T. serpyllum* 'Minimus' is the tiniest and is studded with pink flowers in summer. *T.* 'Goldstream' is similar but has gold-splashed leaves. *T. doerfleri* 'Bressingham' produces its pink flowers particularly freely and *T. serpyllum* var. *albus* bears tiny white blooms. Taller at 4 inches, *T. pulegioides* 'Bertram Anderson' is gold-variegated. Taller still, cultivars of *T. x citriodorus* are generally lemon-scented and include variegated *T. x c.* 'Golden King', a cultivar that is excellent with fish or chicken.

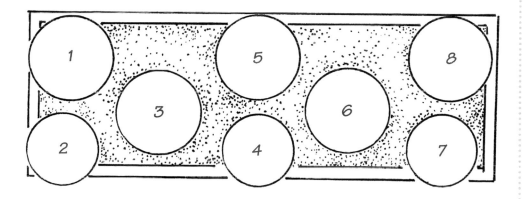

planting key

1 *Thymus × citriodorus*

2 *Thymus pseudolanuginosis*

3 *Thymus vulgaris* 'Silver Posie'

4 *Thymus serpyllum* 'Pink Chintz'

5 *Thymus* 'Fragrantissimus'

6 *Thymus pulegioides* 'Aureus'

7 *Thymus* 'Snowdrift'

8 *Thymus* 'Porlock'

Ice cool

A cool, refreshing scheme for a hot spot, this combination of white and pale blue petunias, dwarf marguerites (*Argyranthemum*) and other white flowers will supply summer-long color.

A clear symmetry adds strength and an air of formality to this arrangement, planted in a lattice-clad wooden window box that has been painted pale blue. In fact, it can be painted to tie in with any color scheme you like, but take care to choose a color that will complement rather overpower the plants.

Center stage is *Argyranthemum frutescens* 'Sugar Button'; the yellow button-like center of each flower is circled by reflexed white petals. On either side of it, *A.* 'Blanche' from the Courtyard Series forms neat, bushy

mounds of blue-green leaves beneath masses of white daisies. In front, the scented white blooms of *Nemesia* 'Innocence' are flanked by a mixture of white and light blue annual petunias.

At each end, *Diascia* 'Ice Cracker' sends up spikes of glistening pure white, while *Sutera cordata* 'Snowflake' spills its trailing stems of bright green leaves and tiny white flowers over the front edge of the window box. For all the plants in the box, remove faded flowerheads regularly and give occasional liquid fertilizer to encourage a succession of blooms.

Other plants for full sun include *Gaura lindheimeri* 'Whirling Butterflies', *Petunia* 'Surfinia White', *Antirrhinum hispanicum* 'Avalanche', *Osteospermum* 'Arctur', *Pelargonium* 'White Blizzard' and *Petunia* 'Million Bells White'. To lift a shady spot, try *Begonia hypolipara* 'Illumination White' and *Impatiens* 'Fiesta White'.

MARGUERITES

Marguerites (*Argyranthemum*) are a large, invaluable group of daisies that, although only half-hardy, flower from early summer to late autumn and often beyond.

Marguerites revel in a sunny spot and enjoy a free-draining soil. They quickly grow into bushy, rounded plants varying in height from 12 to 36 inches or more, and can look especially striking planted as single specimens in matching pots. They can also be trained on short stems to form impressive round-headed standards. In pots, give a dilute liquid feeding every two weeks and remove any faded blooms.

Colors range from the typical yellow-centered white of A. 'Snow Storm', to shades of yellow, pink, near-red and apricot, and their filigree leaves are attractive on their own. Some varieties, such as pink A. 'Summer Melody', bear double flowers. A. 'Vancouver' has unusual pink flowers with double centers surrounded by a single outer row of elongated petals.

A. 'Petite Pink', a compact form growing 12 inches high, is decorated with masses of small, pale pink blooms, while A. 'Peach Cheeks' is peachy-apricot. The yellow-centered white daisies of A. *gracile* 'Chelsea Girl' (pictured above) appear to hover above mounds of feathery leaves. The brightest coloring of all is offered by sunshine-yellow A. 'Jamaica Primrose', a reliable favorite.

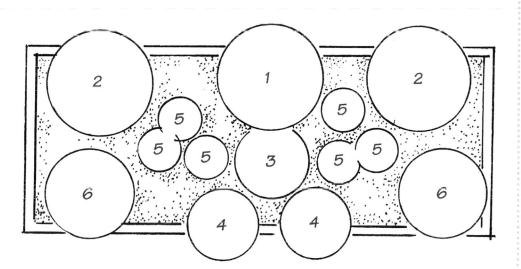

planting key

1 *Argyranthemum frutescens* 'Sugar Button'
2 *Argyranthemum* 'Blanche' (Courtyard Series)
3 *Nemesia* 'Innocence'
4 *Sutera cordata* 'Snowflake'
5 *Petunia* 'Frenzy' light blue and white
6 *Diascia* 'Ice Cracker'

Box of delights

Given a sunny or lightly shaded position, this classic combination of fuchsias, trailing and fancy-leaved pelargoniums, and variegated felicia will flower nonstop for months on end.

Standing proud at the back is *Fuchsia* 'Checkerboard', a vigorous upright variety draped in dainty reddish-pink flowers that are flushed pinkish-white and borne profusely throughout summer and autumn. To each side of the fuchsia is *Pelargonium* 'Frank Headley', a fancy-leaved variety with cream-and-green variegated leaves topped with clusters of salmon-pink flowers. In front, a variegated, stiffly branching *Felicia amelloides* adds its reliable combination of creamy-yellow leaves and bright blue daisy flowers to this busy scene. The less common

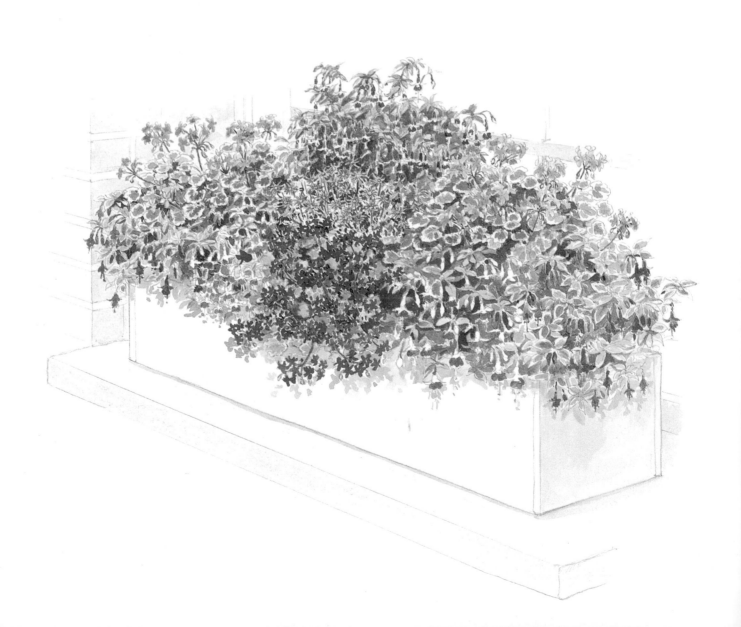

white-flowered variegated form, *F. amelloides*, is also worth seeking out.

At the heart of this concoction is *Pelargonium* 'Red-Blizzard', a trailing variety with clusters of bright red flowers. Completing the front row and softening the lines of the window box are trailing *Fuchsia* 'Lena' and *F.* 'Golden Marinka'. *F.* 'Lena' is the more flowery of the two, with masses of semi-double purple-and-creamy-white blooms. The flowers of *F.* 'Golden Marinka' are dark red, and are emphasized by its leaves, which are marked with golden yellow. Other colored-leaved trailing fuchsias include cream-variegated, red-and-purple flowered *F.* 'Tom West' and fiery *F.* 'Autumnale', whose leaves develop shades of red, orange and gold as they mature. *F.* 'Firecracker' is an upright variety with orange-red tubular flowers and pink, cream and green leaves.

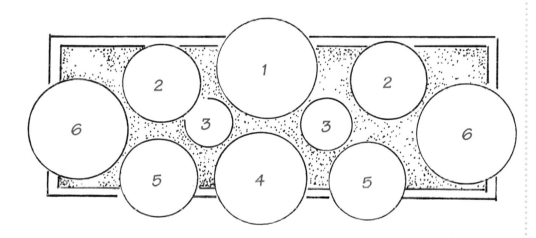

plant close-up

HALF-HARDY PERENNIALS

In recent years the range of half-hardy or tender perennials has increased enormously. They are unsurpassed for their long-flowering ability and they can be kept from year to year provided you can give them a frost-free winter home.

Among them are many daisy-flowered plants including osteospermums and arctotis, and they also include fuchsias, pelargoniums and tuberous-rooted begonias. New cultivars are introduced each year: those listed below are just some of the most suitable for containers. Most prefer full sun, but a few are tolerant of a little shade.

Trailing *Anagallis* 'Skylover' (gentian-blue, pictured above); *Torenia* 'Blue Moon' (pale blue trumpets); *Petunia* 'Surfinia' (shades of pink, blue and white); *Lotus berthelotii* (feathery gray leaves); *Sutera cordata* 'Blizzard' (tiny white flowers) and *S. c.* 'Blue Showers' (lavender).

Semi-trailing *Brachyscome* 'Blue Mist' (mauve-blue daisies); *Lantana camara* (range of two-toned flowerheads including pink/yellow, orange/yellow and orange/red-brown); *Lysimachia congestiflora* 'Outback Sunset' (yellow-and-green leaves) and *Nemesia* 'Mystic Blue' (mauve-blue).

Upright *Angelonia* 'Angel Mist Purple Stripe' (purple and white, tall); *Gazania* 'Christopher Lloyd' (stripey pink) and *G.* 'Yellow Buttons' (double yellow); *Heliotropium* 'Nagano' (purple, cherry-scented); *Osteospermum* 'Orange Symphony' (soft orange) and *Arctotis* x *hybrida* 'Wine' (reddish pink).

Annual delight

The simplest and least expensive way to achieve attractive containers full of colorful flowers is to sow dwarf varieties of hardy annuals directly into the soil mix. They will develop and flower within just a couple of months and, with a little deadheading, will continue to bloom for several weeks.

There are countless varieties to try, a huge proportion of which are overlooked by gardeners who choose half-hardy annuals such as petunias, busy lizzies (*Impatiens*) and fibrous-rooted begonias. Hardy annuals generally have more charm and, requiring no heat, are cheaper and easier to raise from seed. Grown in a plastic trough placed in a large wooden box, they can quickly be replaced by a later planting once flowering ends.

Some varieties of annuals – pot or English marigolds (*Calendula*), godetias and California poppies (*Eschscholzia*) – will look stunning planted *en masse* in single colors, or color-themed. Here we have used small pools of color randomly dotted and repeated around the trough.

Bright blue love-in-a-mist (*Nigella damascena* 'Miss Jekyll') and *Chrysanthemum coronarium* 'Primrose Gem' lend height to the arrangement, although they will be bushier and shorter if pinched back when young, while *Clarkia* 'Amethyst Glow' and mauve cornflowers (*Centaurea cyanus* 'Mauve Queen') tone in well.

Pale lemon and golden-yellow California poppies (*Eschscholzia*) inject vibrancy, in contrast to *Iberis umbellata* 'Appleblossom' and *Lobularia maritima* 'Apricot Shades', which are more subtle.

HARDY ANNUALS

Most hardy annuals are easy to grow from seed, but have a limited flowering period. However, if you sow a succession you will have flowers from late spring to mid-autumn. Come the end of the season, you can harvest your own seed for a free display the following year.

Hardy annuals, such as love-in-a-mist (*Nigella damascena*, pictured above), can be sown any time from early spring to early summer, either outdoors in their flowering positions or in pots, then grown on in a cold frame and eventually planted out into their final containers as young plants. The term "annual" means they will grow, flower, set seed and die within a year or less.

For hanging baskets the flowering period of hardy annuals is generally too short, but in troughs, window boxes and pots, where it is easier to replace them, they are ideal. They are also useful for sprinkling under container-grown shrubs to provide a bright splash of color from plants that will not compete too much with the roots of the shrub for moisture and nutrients.

One of the most rewarding aspects of growing hardy annuals is the fact that the majority will set plenty of seed that can be saved for the following year, or sown in autumn for an early display the following spring. Unless you are going to plant it right away, collect the seed in a paper bag and keep in paper envelopes (marked with the name of the plant and date you collected it) in an airtight container, stored a cool, dark place.

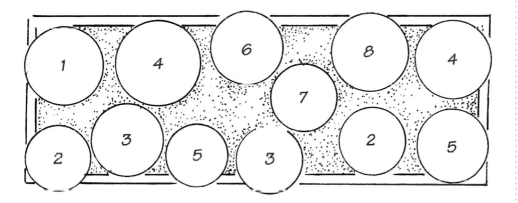

planting key

1 *Iberis umbellata* 'Appleblossom'
2 *Eschscholzia caespitosa* 'Sundew'
3 *Eschscholzia californica* 'Thai Silk Lemon Bush'
4 *Chrysanthemum coronarium* 'Primrose Gem'

5 *Lobularia maritima* 'Apricot Shades'
6 *Nigella damascena* 'Miss Jekyll'
7 *Centaurea cyanus* 'Mauve Queen'
8 *Clarkia* 'Amethyst Glow'

Potted cornfield

This trough is filled with summery cornfield flowers and grasses, bringing the natural beauty of a meadow to your window, balcony or patio. It is a variation of the scheme on pages 86–87.

Made from rustic natural timber and painted in a shade of light brown, this large, accommodating trough suits our potted cornfield perfectly. By siting it in a sunny spot, you can enjoy all the flowers associated with summer meadows. But you don't have to stick slavishly to purely wild species – there is no reason why you shouldn't also use cultivated forms, provided they look right. Here we have mixed the true wild species of some with selected forms or varieties of others, simply because they are more dwarf or more free-flowering.

Sown directly into the trough in a jumble, it is very much a case of survival of the fittest. Most will make it, but some will not. Do not worry: sow a wide selection, and come midsummer you will have a waving mass of leaf and bloom.

Resembling the field poppy but with more ornamental appeal, *Papaver commutatum* 'Lady Bird' bears crimson blooms with a black blotch at the base of each petal. It looks good with the bright yellow daisies of the corn marigold (*Chrysanthemum segetum*). Papery, dwarf blue cornflowers (*Centaurea cyanus* 'Florence Blue'), white ox-eye daisies (*Leucanthemum vulgare*) and pink corncockle (*Agrostemma githago*) add further color. Annual grasses, including hare's tail (*Lagurus ovatus*), squirrel-tail grass (*Hordeum jubatum*) and quaking grass (*Briza maxima*), contribute a welcome tactile element to the "meadow."

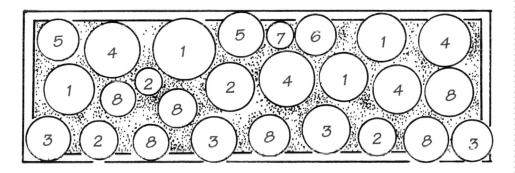

planting key

1 *Chrysanthemum segetum*
2 *Papaver commutatum* 'Lady Bird'
3 *Centaurea cyanus* 'Florence Blue'
4 *Leucanthemum vulgare*
5 *Briza maxima*
6 *Hordeum jubatum*
7 *Lagurus ovatus*
8 *Agrostemma githago*

plant close-up

WILDFLOWERS

Wildflowers are not always suitable for containers because they often flower for only a short time. However, if you would like to grow your own slice of wildflower meadow, containers provide the answer, just on a small scale.

Wildflower seed is best planted as soon as it is ripe, in a mix that mimics the type of soil that is found in the plants' native habitat. By re-creating their preferred conditions as closely as possible, you can grow almost any wildflower successfully in pots or troughs.

Primroses (*Primula vulgaris*), cowslips (*P. veris*), foxgloves (*Digitalis purpurea*) and knapweeds (*Centaurea nigra*) are typical of woodland clearings and are also adept at colonizing sunny banks. Woodland habitats boast wood anemones (*Anemone nemorosa*), bluebells (*Hyancinthoides non-scripta*) and celandines (*Ranunculus ficaria*). In meadows there are mallows (*Malva sylvestris*), cranesbills (*Geranium pratense*), oxlips (*Primula elatior*) and valerian (*Valeriana officinalis*), and coastlines have amazing drought-resistant plants, such as sea pinks (*Armeria maritima*, pictured above) and rock cress (*Arabis alpina*).

You can purchase wildflower seed, plus other species, as small "plugs" or plantlets from specialist nurseries. These are used primarily for establishing wildflower meadows, but there is no reason why your habitat may not be as small as a large container. Never dig up plants growing in the wild.

Modern metal

This stylish and architectural grouping of spiky, drought-tolerant foliage plants includes prickly sea hollies (*Eryngium*) and succulent agaves, and is presented in a pair of shiny metal troughs, mulched with crushed glass – perfect for a contemporary courtyard or a sheltered urban roof garden.

Good drainage is vital for these plants, so make sure there are plenty of holes drilled in the base of the troughs and add a layer of small stones, coarse gravel or terracotta pieces before filling with a gritty, free-draining mix. The troughs are made from stainless steel.

Though they are not frost hardy, agaves will provide a strong summer focal point on a sun-drenched patio and they are the dominant plant in this display. They should

be sited with care to avoid passers-by being scratched by the leaves. The leaves of *Agave americana* are turquoise-green, but for this collection we have chosen *A. a.* 'Mediopicta', which has a central stripe of creamy yellow on each leaf.

Sea hollies (*Eryngium*) require plenty of depth for their long tap roots. Branching stems end in steely-blue pincushions. Succulent *Aeonium* 'Zwartkop' displays contrasting fleshy, ebony-colored leaves, while *Astelia chathamica* forms clumps of silver swords. The woolly first-year rosettes of biennial *Verbascum bombyciferum* 'Polarsommer' resemble silver-gray felt, while *Echeveria secunda* var. *glauca* is an exotic ground cover.

As a finishing touch, the surface of the soil mix has been mulched with crushed recycled glass to echo the reflective qualities of the steel.

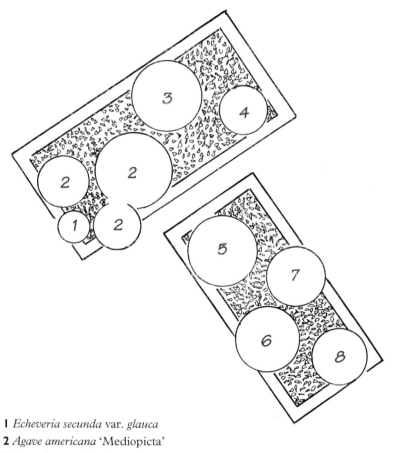

planting key

1 *Echeveria secunda* var. *glauca*
2 *Agave americana* 'Mediopicta'
3 *Eryngium* × *tripartitum*
4 *Aeonium* 'Zwartkop'
5 *Astelia chathamica*
6 *Verbascum bombyciferum* 'Polarsommer'
7 *Eryngium* 'Jos Eijking'
8 *Eryngium agavifolium*

plant close-up

ARCHITECTURAL FOLIAGE

When your garden calls for a bold, dramatic statement, choose from the group of plants that can be loosely termed "architectural." These include many evergreens and quite a few plants that are not frost hardy but will gladly live outdoors while the weather is mild. For that reason, they are handy subjects for pots and can be moved into more sheltered places during the colder months.

These plants work like ornaments, because they have key positions in the layout of the garden. They can be used to create rhythm by repetition or simply provide a little drama at the end of an otherwise dull area.

The sense of drama is generated by the boldness of the foliage and a distinctive outline. The container itself should be simple in style. Agaves, yuccas and phormiums provide an exotic flavor suited to Mediterranean-style gardens, while in a country garden, globe artichokes (*Cynara scolymus*) may be used. In formal gardens, topiary in yew (*Taxus*) or box (*Buxus*) supply structure. Urban situations benefit from the shiny leaves of *Fatsia japonica* or x *Fatshedera lizei* or the jagged effect of *Mahonia* x *media* 'Lionel Fortescue'. On a smaller scale, evergreen euphorbias that are useful in a variety of settings include *E. characias* subsp. *wulfenii* (pictured above) and the more compact *E. c.* subsp. *characias* 'Humpty Dumpty'.

Daisy, daisy

When it comes to simple beauty, few plants surpass daisies – and the daisy family includes a plethora of different genera, a considerable number of which succeed well in containers.

Half-hardy perennial daisies such as osteospermums can be persuaded to flower almost continuously for several months if given a sunny position and fertilized, deadheaded and watered regularly. This summery show incorporates pale yellow, stiffly upright-growing *Osteospermum* 'Buttermilk' and the more lax-stemmed, buttery-yellow *O.* 'Lemon Symphony'. Both open their well-formed blooms wide on a warm, sunny day and close up in the evening to reveal metallic undersides.

Another large group of daisies, the marguerites

(*Argyranthemum*), are represented in this line-up by *A*. 'Vanilla Ripple' a creamy-yellow cultivar that blooms abundantly and indefinitely. To add a little fizz to this pale and understated color combination we have called on *Arctotis × hybrida* 'Red Devil', a stunning variety of Zulu daisy. Dotted among the other bushier plants, its slender, silvery stems proudly support large blooms of a near-metallic orange-red that open flat in the sun.

The golden-yellow blooms of *Pallenis maritima*, resembling gold coins, continue the brighter theme on compact plants.

Swan river daisy (*Brachyscome multifida*) spills over the edge of the metal trough in a burst of fresh green filigree leaves speckled with small mauve, yellow-centered daisies. As an alternative edging, consider mixing in coarser-leaved *B*. 'Strawberry Mousse', with its flowers the color of crushed strawberries.

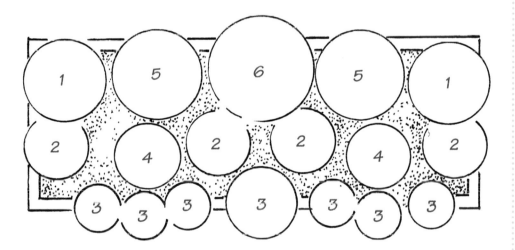

planting key

1 *Osteospermum* 'Lemon Symphony'
2 *Arctotis × hybrida* 'Red Devil'
3 *Brachyscome multifida*
4 *Pallenis maritima*
5 *Argyranthemum* 'Vanilla Ripple'
6 *Osteospermum* 'Buttermilk'

plant close-up

OSTEOSPERMUMS

Osteospermums hail from South Africa where they flourish in open, well-drained grassland and on forest margins.

Reveling in well-drained soil and full sun, osteospermums will flower continuously for weeks if deadheaded occasionally, blooming in a range of colors. Some, such as pale yellow *O.* 'Buttermilk', grow distinctly upright to about 24 inches, while others, like pale mauve *O.* 'Cannington Roy', are prostrate, achieving only 6 inches in height but spreading to 24 inches across. Their petals have undersides that are often as highly colored as their upper surface, visible when they close in the evening.

In the open garden, a few varieties, most notably *O. jucundum* and its forms, will survive several degrees of frost, although above ground and in containers they will need plenty of protection. In areas prone to frost, the less hardy perennial kinds are best regarded as annuals or overwintered as cuttings taken in summer.

Among the best osteospermums are *O.* 'Stardust' (deep purple-pink and frost hardy); *O.* 'Orange Symphony' (semi-prostrate, bright orange), *O.* 'Whirlygig' (silvery white with spoon-shaped petals, pictured above); *O.* 'Silver Sparkler' (white flowers, creamy-white edged leaves) and *O.* 'Nairobi Purple' (deep purple, low-growing).

Harvest

Cozy autumn days are reflected in this harvest festival of dwarf chrysanthemums, ornamental kale (*Brassica oleracea*) and the papery orange fruit of the Chinese lantern (*Physalis alkekengi*).

Although many plants bloom more sparsely, if at all, as the weather cools down, chrysanthemums really come into their own when summer blends into autumn. The dwarf kinds are the most useful for containers and we have used two varieties from the appropriately named Showmaker Series.

Chrysanthemum 'Showmaker Action' is a double-flowered cultivar bearing masses of orange-bronze blooms with golden-yellow highlights. The double, multi-petaled blooms of *C.* 'Showmaker Chorus' are

deep, rich pink. There are numerous others in shades ranging from clear yellow to bronze-red. All are suited to terracotta containers such as the rough-textured trough we have used here.

The other main stars of this crowded planting are jagged-leaved ornamental kales (*Brassica oleracea* 'Kale White Peacock'), with leaves that turn more obviously creamy-white or pink-flushed, as they develop.

A final touch of bright orange is provided by *Physalis alkekengi* var. *franchetii*. Commonly known as Chinese lantern, it bears red fruit encased in large, papery calyces that resemble hanging lanterns. It can either be planted in the trough or added as dried stems pushed in at the back. In fact, there is no reason why you shouldn't pep up any of your containers by adding dried cut flowers, stems or berries to them.

DWARF CHRYSANTHEMUMS

Dwarf chrysanthemums burst into bloom in the latter half of the summer and continue well into autumn. Many have been bred to address the shortage of autumn flowers. Known collectively as 'Charm' chrysanthemums, they are easily grown from young plants purchased in the spring and grown on through the summer, or even from seed, and are available in a range of rich colors. They are short and neat, spreading to form wide cushions just 12–18 inches high. The fact that they become wreathed in flowers, hiding the (not unattractive) leaves, endears them to container gardeners everywhere.

To ensure maximum bushiness, pinch out the growing tips at an early stage and again a little later on. After the plants have flowered, cut them back and move them to a sheltered place, where they will survive the winter in milder areas.

Charm chrysanthemums vary in flower shape, size and color. The yellow-centered single blooms of bronze-red *C.* 'Trapeze', lilac-pink *C.* 'Foxtrot' (pictured above) and yellow *C.* 'Impressario' are relatively dainty, but those of orange-red *C.* 'Crimson Gala', bright yellow *C.* 'Firecracker' and orange-bronze *C.* 'Laureate' are fully double and packed with petals. From a mid-spring sowing, *C.* 'Charm Early Fashion Mixed' produces low cushions in all colors except blue, from late summer until the first frost.

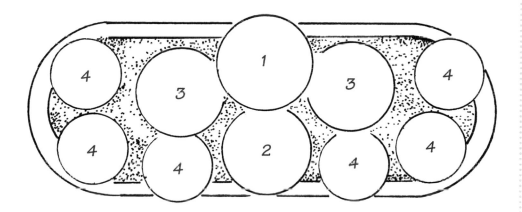

planting key

1 *Physalis alkekengi* var. *franchetii*
2 *Chrysanthemum* 'Showmaker Chorus'
3 *Chrysanthemum* 'Showmaker Action'
4 *Brassica oleracea* 'Kale White Peacock'

Autumn mist

This rather muted, natural-looking collection of autumn plants includes hardy geraniums, displaying autumn leaf color, gracefully fading grasses and autumn-flowering "naked ladies" (*Colchicum*). Clad with rustic logs for a natural look, the container adds to the informality of the planting, a contrast to that on pages 94–95.

At the back, *Pennisetum alopecuroides* 'Hameln' forms a fountain of feathery tails from late summer on. A compact variety of fountain grass, its dark green leaves turn bright yellow in autumn. More upright are the graceful flower spikes of the kaffir lily (*Schizostylis coccinea*), which thrust skyward from early autumn on and erupt into bright red, saucer-shaped blooms. A small drift of the large, pinkish-purple flowers of

Colchicum 'Waterlily' fill out the center of the trough. Their goblet-shaped blooms open wide to reveal a mass of delicate petals.

Two more grasses add their distinctive contribution to the display. First there is *Imperata cylindrica* 'Rubra', with erect bright green, slightly yellowish leaves that become increasingly suffused with deep blood-red as summer progresses, looking especially magical when brightly backlit

by the sun. A useful dwarf grass, it grows just 16 inches high. Cascading over the front, evergreen *Carex comans* 'Frosted Curls' looks good all year; its gently arching, minty-green leaves offer a wonderful foil to a wide variety of plants.

Completing the front row is *Cotoneaster congestus* 'Nanus', which is studded in autumn with glistening red berries, and *Geranium dalmaticum,* with attractive leaves that develop red tints.

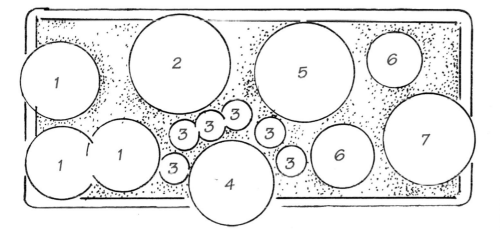

plant close-up

AUTUMN BULBS

Blooming at a time when the focus of attention shifts from flowers to berries and temporary leaf coloring, autumn bulbs are a more than welcome reassurance that there are still plenty of flowers to be found late in the year.

Best known of the autumn bulbs are the colchicums. Commonly called "naked ladies," due to the fact that they produce their elegant goblet-shaped blooms far ahead of the leaves, they resemble crocuses but are much larger in flower and leaf. Reveling in a sunny, well-drained position, they should be planted 4–6 inches deep in late summer, as soon as the corms are available. They will be in bloom within a matter of weeks. *Colchicum autumnale* is the most readily available, its 6-inch-high goblets are a pale pinkish lilac, except in the form *C. a.* 'Album', which is pure white. There are a few double-flowered colchicums, including *C.* 'Waterlily' used in the container opposite.

Crocuses are another important group of autumn-flowering bulbs. They are ideal for growing in pots in full sun, where they will spring into bloom in late autumn. The saffron crocus (*C. sativus*) bears large lilac blooms, while those of *C. speciosus* can be purple, mauve or white. *C. kotschyanus* (pictured above) sends up its lilac-pink flowers earlier than most, in early autumn.

Not often seen in pots outdoors, nerines are stunning in flower. In mid-autumn, *N. bowdenii* bears small clusters of bright pink blooms.

Hanging baskets

Hanging baskets first appeared as something of a gardening novelty, but they quickly caught on and have become steadily more popular over the past few decades. There are endless products that are now widely available to make the job of caring for them as easy as possible, and few would disagree that a well-planted and tended hanging basket in full flower is a truly spectacular sight.

Growing plants in hanging baskets is the only form of gardening that does not involve using any ground space – they need only air space, so are especially favored by those with little or even no garden at all. Buildings and walls of all types can be instantly and dramatically improved by the addition of these suspended, living plant arrangements. And, when teamed with matching pots, window boxes and wall baskets, they are supremely eye-catching.

Besides the more obvious and popular half-hardy annuals and tender perennials, a wide range of plants can be grown successfully in hanging baskets; in fact, everything from herbs and vegetables to alpines and heathers. Hanging baskets are also the perfect way to show off plants with long trails of flowers and foliage, tumbling grasses and lax fruiting plants such as tomatoes and strawberries. What is more, all sorts of containers can be recycled as hanging baskets; try old buckets and saucepans, small birdcages, shopping baskets and colanders. The only limitation is your own resourcefulness.

By taking care of a few basic requirements – most notably watering, fertilizing, and choosing the right plant for the right place – beautiful hanging baskets brimming with blooms are well within everyone's grasp.

Spring medley

The palette of spring plants suitable for hanging baskets is limited, but with imagination it is still possible to grow an excellent display. This cheery mixture heralds the spring with reliable pansies (*Viola* x *wittrockiana*) in a riotous clash of colors and various dwarf shrubs and ground-cover plants.

Plants that flower in spring tend to do so with enthusiasm. Pansies are a shining example, but you still need plants with interesting foliage to bulk up the display and supplement the flowers. Planted in autumn, this basket provides interest through winter, but in spring, when the daffodils bloom and the pansies flower freely, it peaks. Contained in an open-sided mesh basket lined with moss, the plants will be at the mercy of the

winter weather, and although hardy they will still be susceptible to damage from cold, drying winds. Consequently, place the completed basket in as sheltered a position as possible.

As winter approaches, plant growth slows, so plant winter and spring baskets far more densely than summer ones to achieve a mature effect. The centerpiece here is purple sage (*Salvia officinalis* 'Purpurascens'), an aromatic evergreen that forms an excellent backdrop. Multi-headed *Narcissus* 'Tête-à-tête' and *N.* 'February Silver' rise above the other plants in a blaze of yellow and white, while cream-variegated *Aubrieta* 'Doctor Mules Variegata' opens its mauve-purple blooms later. Creamy-white variegated *Vinca minor* 'Argenteovariegata' and *Hedera helix* 'Eva' trail their stems over the sides, contrasting well with dark-leaved *Ajuga reptans* 'Braunherz'.

VIOLAS AND PANSIES

Eternally popular as container plants, violas and pansies (*Viola* x *wittrockiana*) can – aided by fertilizing, watering and removing faded blooms – flower for months on end. In fact, with winter-flowering kinds, it is possible to have violas in flower in every month of the year.

Pansies are cultivars of *Viola* x *wittrockiana*, a hybrid resulting from cross-breeding several viola species including *V. cornuta* and the wild pansy, or heartsease (*V. tricolor*).

Although perennial, pansies are generally treated as biennials or annuals. Other violas are regarded as perennials, but their lives are limited in pots. A large range of pansy and viola seed is available, but individually named varieties grow best from cuttings taken in spring or summer. The plants thrive in sun or light shade – they become more drawn and leggy the shadier it is. Cut back untidy plants; it's hard to rejuvenate them.

Among the named cultivars, *V.* 'Irish Molly' is an unusual golden brown and *V.* 'Jackanapes' a cheery combination of purple and sunshine-yellow. *V. sororia* 'Freckles' (pictured above) has white blooms, heavily speckled with purple. The horned violet (*V. cornuta*) is an evergreen perennial bearing lavender-blue blooms.

Of the numerous pansy seed mixtures available, the winter-flowering Ultima Series offers a wide range of colors. The spring- and summer-flowering Clear Crystal Series has clear colors without the typical contrasting markings.

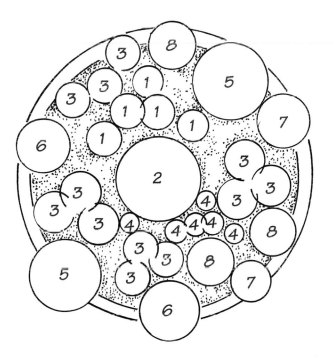

planting key

1 *Narcissus* 'February Silver'
2 *Salvia officinalis* 'Purpurascens'
3 *Viola* × *wittrockiana* Ultima Series mixed
4 *Narcissus* 'Tête-à-tête'
5 *Hedera helix* 'Eva'
6 *Aubrieta* 'Doctor Mules Variegata'
7 *Vinca minor* 'Argenteovariegata'
8 *Ajuga reptans* 'Braunherz'

High-rise succulents

For dramatic, year-round effect, this tufa rock hosts a collection of houseleeks (*Sempervivum*). There are dozens of varieties, all forming fleshy, symmetrical rosettes in varying colors and textures. Their red, pink or yellow flowers are a striking addition in summer. A range of other alpine and rock garden plants – lime-loving

saxifrages (*Saxifraga*) in particular – are good alternatives that would work just as well.

Tufa is a lightweight, porous limestone that absorbs and retains moisture, and is ideal for housing tiny alpines and plants that thrive where soil is shallow or almost non-existent. Suspended from a low wall bracket, even small

pieces of tufa add height and interest to a collection of alpines, succulents and cacti.

To plant into tufa rock, drill or chisel pockets at least 4 inches deep and 1–2 inches diameter. Drill side pockets at an angle and those on horizontal surfaces straight down. Soak the tufa overnight and drop a little sharp sand into each hole before adding soil mix. Choose young plants or offsets and wash the roots clean of old soil before inserting

them into the pockets. Use a dibbler or a pencil to firm more soil around them. Add small chips of tufa to wedge the plants in place.

If you cannot obtain tufa or afford a sizable piece, achieve a similar effect by planting into a small, moss-lined hanging basket and place some weathered rock pieces in the top. Ground-covering stonecrops (*Sedum*) and houseleeks will quickly colonize the basket.

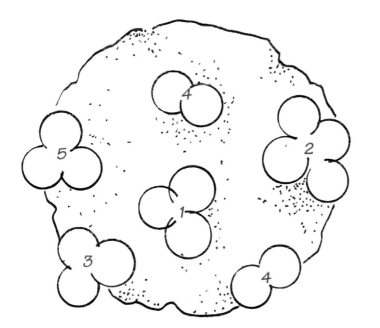

planting key

1 *Sempervivum arachnoideum*
2 *Sempervivum* 'Commander Hay'
3 *Sempervivum giuseppii*
4 *Sempervivum montanum*
5 *Sempervivum tectorum*

plant close-up

SUCCULENTS

Whether on a scorching, sun-drenched patio where other plants would dry out too quickly, or in containers that tend to be watered infrequently, fleshy-leaved succulent plants are well equipped to deal with hot, dry conditions. They naturally store water in their leaves, stems, branches or roots during rainy spells, and are supremely able to cope with periods of drought.

This diverse, dramatic-looking plant group also encompasses the often strikingly colorful (though not frost hardy) cacti. Their unusual appearance and easy-going nature ensures they are also popular with children.

Houseleeks (*Sempervivum*, pictured above) and stonecrops (*Sedum*) are native to temperate climates; they are frost hardy. A large proportion of cacti and succulents, however, are native to semi-arid regions of Central and South America, so in most areas they will need to winter indoors. Agaves, aeoniums and echeverias are among these. Grouped together they form striking contrasts of habit and texture.

Succulents suit any size of container, even very shallow ones. Choose one that enhances the shape and texture of the plants. Shallow bowls, for instance, suit low-growing, creeping or rosette-forming types, while taller, branching succulents like aeoniums make stunning solitary specimens in curvaceous olive jars. Above all, use a free-draining gritty compost and do not allow them to become waterlogged, especially in winter.

Color ball

It is amazing how effective a basket of just one type of plant can be, whether in a single color or as a mixture of shades. Pools of color created by "mono" hanging baskets achieve the greatest visual impact possible, drawing the eye to them with unfailing ease – whether willingly or otherwise.

To create a real ball of color, it is best to use an open-sided mesh basket and plant through the sides, although this really depends on the type of plant you are intending to use. Many plants have such a strongly trailing habit that they will hide the sides of an enclosed hanging pot in no time at all. These include trailing begonias, fuchsias and pelargoniums. In fact, it's better to confine some plants – most notably trailing petunias –

to their own designated basket, because they are so vigorous that they will quickly engulf less rampant plants.

The most densely planted of the three baskets shown here is filled with *Impatiens* Fiesta Series 'Lavender Orchid', a double-flowered pink busy lizzie. Impatiens have long been used for mono hanging baskets: pinch them back regularly to ensure bushy growth and good coverage. In the neighboring basket, *Pelargonium* 'Blizzard Pink' forms a cascade of blooms. Just five plants will fill a 12-inch basket if planted early in the season. The complementary colors of deep velvety-red *Verbena* 'Diamond Merci', purple-blue *V.* 'Diamond Topaz' and pink *V.* 'Diamond Butterfly' combine luxuriously to fill the third basket.

Experiment with simple combinations of just two or three types of plant in one basket, which can also be stunning.

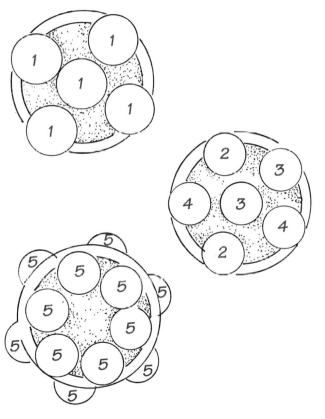

planting key

1 *Pelargonium* 'Blizzard Pink'
2 *Verbena* 'Diamond Merci'
3 *Verbena* 'Diamond Topaz'
4 *Verbena* 'Diamond Butterfly'
5 *Impatiens* Fiesta Series 'Lavender Orchid'

plant close-up

HALF-HARDY ANNUALS

Once the staple of all summer container displays, half-hardy annuals are heavily relied upon for long-lasting flower color. Regular deadheading, and in some cases – petunias, for example – occasional pinching, ensures they flower for several months until caught by the first frosts.

French and African marigolds (*Tagetes*) in yellow, orange and bronze are among the most reliable, as are trumpet-flowered petunias in a wide variety of colors and flower sizes. While most appreciate full sun, busy lizzies (*Impatiens*, pictured above) and fibrous-rooted begonias thrive in shade. The former are available in a wide range of pink, red and orange shades, while the latter have either green or bronze leaves and pink, red or white blooms. An extensive breeding program has resulted in superior varieties known as F1 hybrids that, although expensive, are uniform in height and flower color and compact in habit, guaranteeing long-lasting displays.

Plants grown as half-hardy annuals mature, flower and produce seed in a single season. Many are technically perennial, but they are generally discarded at the end of the season. They require higher germination temperatures than hardy annuals and should be sown in artificial heat, then planted out when all danger of frost has passed. They can be purchased pre-germinated from mail-order companies and garden centers. More advanced "plugs" and young plants are also widely available from mid- to late spring.

On the trail

Often overlooked for containers, many climbers grown as annuals make excellent subjects. Most will flower all summer and they can be trained on frames or allowed to trail naturally.

This rampant mixture includes black-eyed-Susan (*Thunbergia alata*), a popular greenhouse plant bearing orange, cream or yellow blooms with dark centers. Look out for *T. a.* 'Blushing Susie', an unusual seed mixture boasting blooms in less typical shades of strawberry-pink, salmon, ivory and apricot. Scrambling through it is the Chilean glory vine (*Eccremocarpus scaber*), a fast grower that bears massed clusters of narrow, trumpet-shaped flowers in shades of red, orange and yellow for months on end. In frost-free areas it is perennial in the

border, but in containers it is best treated as an annual. Continuing the orange theme is *Ipomoea lobata*, a relative of morning glory with spikes of tiny, banana-shaped blooms that begin orange-red and gradually fade to cream, creating a tropical, multi-colored effect.

Down at the other end of the color spectrum the purple bell vine (*Rhodochiton atrosanguineus*) weaves its way through the other plants to complete this exotic, colorful, flowing planting. Its trailing stems drip with purple-red blooms that have near-black, protruding centers. Straying stems can be tied or woven in, or can be cut back to encourage bushier growth.

Each plant will work equally well on its own and quickly fill a basket with long-lasting color. One container planted with just rhodochiton, for example, is fantastic.

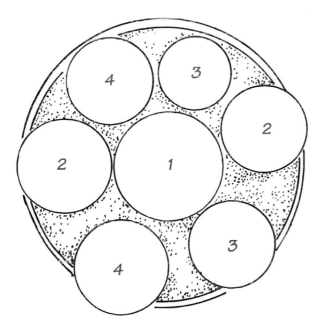

planting key

1 *Ipomoea lobata*
2 *Eccremocarpus scaber*
3 *Thunbergia alata*
4 *Rhodochiton atrosanguineus*

plant close-up

ANNUAL CLIMBERS

Easily raised from seed, annual climbers are the perfect way to achieve height among a collection of containers within a short time span. If sown early in the year, most annual climbers will reach 6 feet or more by midsummer.

By selecting varieties of similar vigor, planting them in a large pot or basket, and allowing them to scramble over a plant support, lovely combinations of leaf and flower can be achieved.

Most popular and widely grown of all annual climbers are sweet peas (*Lathyrus odoratus*), valued for their scent and as cut flowers. Like all annual climbers, they like as deep a pot as possible and enjoy a cool, moist root area.

Morning glories (*Ipomoea*) are another invaluable group, with heart-shaped leaves and trumpet-like flowers that open early in the day but fade before evening. Although they appreciate a warm, sheltered spot, their flowers will last longer in light shade. *I. tricolor* 'Heavenly Blue' bears azure-blue flowers, paling to white at their centers. The blooms of *I. t.* 'Flying Saucers' are marbled white and purple-mauve. *I. t.* 'Star of Yelta' (pictured above) is purple with pinkish-red centers and *I. nil* 'Scarlet O'Hara' is cerise-pink. *I.* 'Mini Sky Blue' has comparatively tiny trumpets.

Ideal for a sheltered, sunny site is *I. quamoclit* with its bright scarlet flowers and handsome leaves. For similar conditions, *Lablab purpureus* is a pea relative with fragrant white or purplish-pink flowers and purplish leaves.

Summer profusion

Unashamedly bright and gaudy, no attempt has been made at subtlety or careful color coordination in this blend of quintessential summer flowers, tailored to a sunny position.

A 16-inch open-sided mesh basket is required to house this number of plants, and even then it is likely to quickly overflow with flowers and foliage. Lined with traditional moss, plants are pushed through the sides and the planting built up in three distinct layers.

At its very heart, standing proud in the center of the top layer, is *Pelargonium* 'Crystal Palace Gem', a vibrant performer with green-and-yellow variegated leaves and salmon-orange blooms. Surrounding it are *Petunia* 'Million Bells Cherry', with small red trumpets, double-

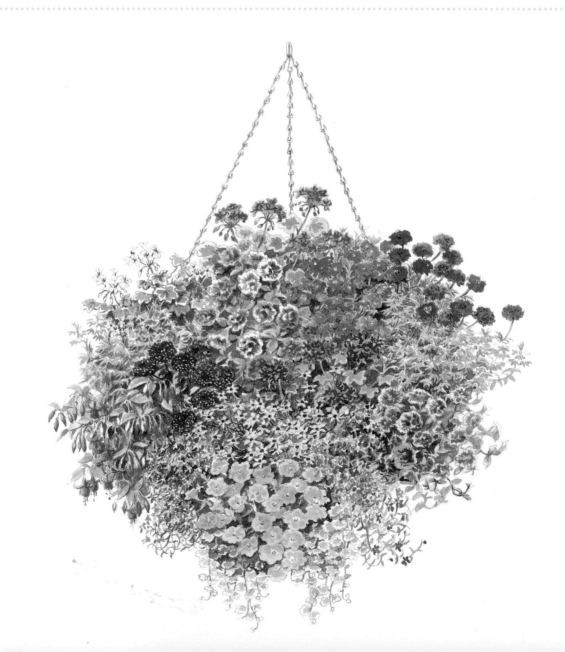

flowered mauve-lilac *P.* 'Priscilla' from the Tumbelina Series and *Verbena* 'Temari Scarlet'. Two reliable trailing pelargoniums also put in an appearance: *P.* 'L'Elégante' for its silvery-mauve blooms and ivy-like, cream-variegated leaves, and deep velvety-red *P.* 'Yale'. Gracing the top edge of the basket are feathery-leaved *Bidens ferulifolia* with bright yellow daisy flowers and *Scaevola aemula* 'Blue Wonder', a lavender-blue trailer with fleshy leaves and fan-shaped flowers. A few wisps of trailing lobelia in blue, pink and red fill out the upper layer.

In the middle layer, *Verbena* 'Lanai Purple' and *Fuchsia* 'Jack Shahan' are joined by variegated mint (*Mentha suaveolens* 'Variegata') and trailing *Petunia* 'Surfinia Sky Blue'.

The lowest layer is composed of more mixed trailing lobelia, which gradually becomes obscured by the upper layers.

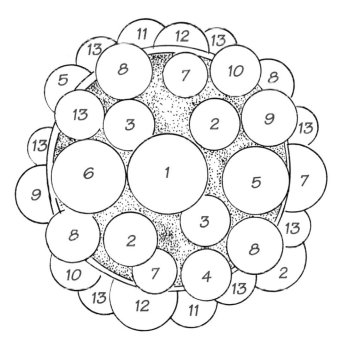

1 *Pelargonium* 'Crystal Palace Gem'
2 *Petunia* 'Priscilla'
3 *Petunia* 'Million Bells Cherry'
4 *Pelargonium* 'Yale'
5 *Verbena* 'Temari Scarlet'
6 *Pelargonium* 'L'Elégante'
7 *Bidens ferulifolia*

8 *Scaevola aemula* 'Blue Wonder'
9 *Verbena* 'Lanai Purple'
10 *Fuchsia* 'Jack Shahan'
11 *Mentha suaveolens* 'Variegata'
12 *Petunia* 'Surfinia Sky Blue'
13 *Lobelia erinus* mixed

plant close-up

PELARGONIUMS

For sheer versatility, variety and flowering ability, pelargoniums are unsurpassed by any other summer-flowering container plant. Flowers range from bright scarlet-red through every shade of pink to white, and in habit from lax trailers to upright, bushy varieties and diminutive miniatures.

All of the literally hundreds of cultivars relish a sunny position and cope well with dry conditions. Easily grown from cuttings, they will need winter protection in frost-prone areas.

The largest group is the "zonal" type. Their leaves are generally rounded and most have "zones" of a darker color. The flowers, held on stout stems above the foliage, can be single, semi-double or fully double. The leaves may be as showy – if not showier – than the flowers. These "fancy-leaved" pelargoniums include such varieties as *P.* 'Contrast', *P.* 'Happy Thought' and *P.* 'Mr. Henry Cox'. 'Stellar' varieties have starry flowers and pointed leaves; all are compact and free-flowering. *P.* 'Strawberry Fayre' bears pinkish-red blooms that pale to white near their centers, while *P.* 'Bird Dancer' (pictured above) is dainty with spidery, pale pink blooms above dark leaves.

"Ivy-leaved" pelargoniums, the other main group, are valued for their trailing leaves and massed flowers. Finally, "scented-leaved" pelargoniums have aromatic foliage. *P.* 'Lady Plymouth' has variegated, deeply divided leaves with a eucalyptus scent. In contrast, *P.* 'Mabel Grey' has green leaves that are lemon-scented.

Summer shady profusion

Finding the most suitable plants to cope with certain conditions takes a little time and effort – in the same way that plants in the open garden have their particular likes and dislikes, those in hanging baskets do, too. This variation on the basket on pages 108–109 features plants that are more tolerant of shade.

Impatiens (busy lizzies) have come a long way in the past 20 years. Far from the lanky specimens they once were, they are now one of the most popular of all bedding plants. In hot sun they wilt in the middle of the day and pick up in the evening. But if you plant them in a cooler, shadier spot, they will perform well all day long, day in, day out.

The various colors in the Accent Series are

particularly useful, and the 'Chelsea' mixture includes a variety of pink shades that complement the pale trailing fuchsias used here: *Fuchsia* 'Annabel' is a large double white, flushed with pink, while *F.* 'Quasar' is another double with blooms of white and pale lavender-blue.

Begonias also prefer to be kept on the cool side in summer. Although they will tolerate full sun, their growth is generally more lush and their flowers more profuse if they are shielded during the hottest part of the day. All the flowers in this basket are large and showy, and the double blooms of *Begonia* 'Illumination Salmon Pink', and *B.* 'Illumination Apricot' are certainly no exception.

Finally, *Sutera* (Bacopa) 'Olympic Gold', although brightest in full sun, adds its yellow-green leaves and white flowers to the lowest tier, helping to complete an opulent, chandelier effect.

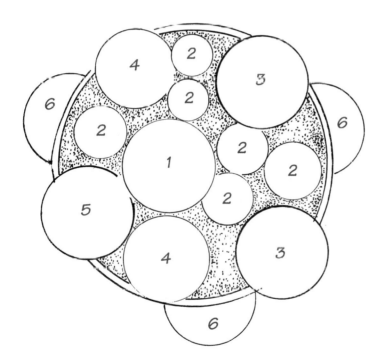

planting key

1 *Fuchsia* 'Annabel'
2 *Impatiens* Accent 'Chelsea' mixed
3 *Begonia* 'Illumination Apricot'
4 *Fuchsia* 'Quasar'
5 *Begonia* 'Illumination Salmon Pink'
6 *Sutera* (Bacopa) 'Olympic Gold'

plant close-up

FUCHSIAS

There are few plants as versatile as fuchsias. The trailing varieties drape their lax stems laden with blooms, while the upright types can form a striking centerpiece. A group of a single variety looks particularly effective, and fuchsias trained as fans, standards or pillars are a guaranteed conversation piece.

For relatively little effort, fuchsias will give an elegant, summer-long display year after year. They prefer a cool position and consistently moist soil, but are remarkably tolerant otherwise.

Among the best trailing doubles are *F.* 'Dancing Flame' (orange), *F.* 'Blue Veil' (white and pale lavender), and *F.* 'Swingtime' (red and white). Singles include *F.* 'Red Spider' (deep crimson), *F.* 'Eva Boerg' (violet purple and white, pictured above), and *F.* 'Auntie Jinks' (pinkish purple and creamy white).

Upright bush varieties of particular merit include *F.* 'Waltz Jubelteen' (candy-pink blooms), *F.* 'Dark Eyes' (purple and red), *F.* 'Ting-a-ling' (single white), *F.* 'Leonora' (pale pink) and *F.* 'Celia Smedley' (white and rose-pink).

Easily grown from cuttings taken in summer, most fuchsias require frost protection in winter, although single-flowered bush types are generally hardier.

Afternoon tea

This confection of sun-loving summer flowers in pale cream, pink and strawberry-red looks good enough to eat. Included here are diascias, trailing snapdragons (*Antirrhinum*) and cream petunias.

Hardy perennial *Heuchera* 'Chocolate Ruffles' makes a strong centerpiece, its large scalloped leaves purple-red above and beet-red below. Many hardy perennials and dwarf shrubs grown for their foliage make excellent central plants for large hanging baskets.

Skirting the heuchera is a mixture of petunias and a collection of pink-flowered diascias. *D.* 'Pink Panther' has spikes of soft pink blooms with pronounced deep pink centers, while *D.* Redstart is the closest to a red *diascia* so far available. *D. barberae* 'Ruby Field' is an

older, frost-hardy variety widely planted in rock gardens and as a border edging. Its rosy-pink blooms are produced on short spikes throughout the summer.

Two more trailing plants hide the sides of the basket. *Antirrhinum hispanicum* 'Avalanche' has a gently cascading habit and bears white snapdragon-like flowers with yellow central markings. The silver-gray leaves set off the flowers to perfection. In the lower section of the basket, a ring of *Sutera* 'Lavender Storm' sends long, branching stems earthbound, covered with tiny leaves and equally dainty lavender-blue flowers.

Although not strictly conforming to the color scheme, *Cuphea llavea* 'Georgia Scarlet' (syn. *C. l.* 'Tiny Mice') completes the effect. The tip of each semi-trailing stem ends with a small cluster of purple-and-red blooms that, on close inspection, resemble the faces of mice.

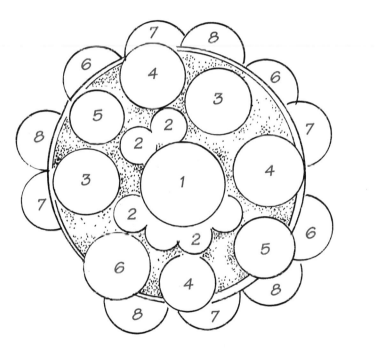

plant close-up

DIASCIAS

Diascias are creeping, mat-forming, sun-loving perennials from South Africa that are invaluable as container plants. Their long flowering season and delightful color range has endeared diascias to gardeners everywhere. In summer they produce short spikes of small but distinctive flowers that are divided into five lobes. Each has a wide lower lobe and upper lobes formed in pairs. The upper lobes are backed by long spurs that add to the flowers' flamboyant appearance.

New varieties continue to be introduced, although some of the older species and cultivars remain popular. One of the taller species, *D. rigescens*, has densely packed flower spikes of deep pink, while cultivars *D. barberae* 'Blackthorn Apricot' and *D.* 'Salmon Supreme' (pictured above) are shorter and colored according to their names. *D.* 'Ice Cracker' is a good pure white, while *D.* 'Little Dancer' is one of the shortest and most free-flowering of all, forming bright pink mounds.

Diascias thrive in moist but well-drained soil in full sun. Some survive a few degrees of frost, but most are less hardy and all resent excessive winter wetness. In summer, they can quickly outgrow smaller pots and look sick. Rejuvenate by cutting back hard and applying a general-purpose liquid fertilizer. Because of their creeping nature, and habit of rooting as they spread, propagate by dividing established plants in spring or summer. Or, take tip cuttings from non-flowering shoots in summer.

A bowl of roses

Even relatively large-growing plants can be used in hanging baskets in the short term. Small shrubs, conifers and climbing plants will all succeed for a while, until they become potbound and outgrow their allotted space. Ground-cover roses are a good example. Unlike their bushy counterparts, they will survive in **large hanging baskets for a few years if kept well watered, fed and pruned.**

Here a pair of large, hayrack-style wall baskets are used to provide as much room for the rose roots as possible. They are lined with cocoa-fiber matting, but other suitable linings include foam, moss and black plastic with drainage

holes. Each wall basket is planted with a single ground-cover rose from the 'County' range. Ground-cover roses have a lax, malleable habit, so besides trailing over the basket edges, they can be trained on a piece of trellis to cover the wall itself.

A dense shrub growing just 12 inches high but spreading to 32 inches across, *Rosa* 'Hampshire' bears single bright scarlet blooms in profusion throughout the summer and autumn. Each flower displays prominent golden-yellow stamens and as an added bonus blooms are followed by orange-red hips in autumn. By contrast, *R.* 'Sussex' bears large trusses of double apricot-buff blooms on its gracefully arching branches.

When they eventually become tired and untidy, rejuvenate in autumn or early spring. Lift the plants out of the baskets, shake off the soil, and prune the roots before replanting in fresh mix.

GROUND-COVER ROSES

An innovation of recent years, ground-cover roses are suited to growing in large containers, where they can be left to trail informally or trained more formally over a support.

Among the best are those in the 'County' range (*Rosa* 'Sussex' is pictured above), bred to be repeat-blooming and thereby ensure a long flowering period. Colors range from pure white through pink and yellow to red, and the flowers can be single, double or semi-double. *R.* 'Avon' bears double blooms that are blush-pink in bud opening to white, while vigorous *R.* 'Gwent' will need more controlling than most but displays double lemon-yellow flowers over a long period. *R.* 'Rutland' is daintier with soft pink blooms and *R.* 'Northamptonshire' is creamy white.

Most ground-cover roses are sparsely thorny, but care should still be taken to site them where they will not be a danger to passersby. Prune and tie in long shoots to limit the problem. For added interest in summer, annual climbing plants such as canary creeper (*Tropaeolum peregrinum*) and purple bell vine (*Rhodochiton atrosanguineus*) can be allowed to scramble through the roses.

To get the best from them, place in a sunny or lightly shaded position and feed occasionally with a specific rose fertilizer. Remove faded flower stems, pruning back to an emergent bud. Watch out for aphids and spray at the first sign of attack. Prune established plants to a strong framework of outward-facing buds in late winter or early spring.

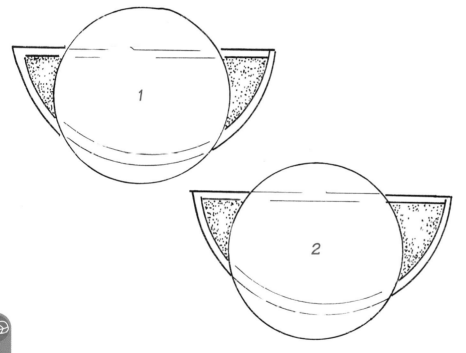

planting key

1 *Rosa* 'Hampshire'
2 *Rosa* 'Sussex'

Herbal basket

Herbs have long been grown in containers, placed conveniently close to the kitchen. They can look especially effective in hanging baskets, where they take up no ground space yet still provide the necessary ingredients to spice up a variety of culinary dishes or offer natural cures for various common ailments.

Planted in a plastic-lined wicker or rattan basket with drainage holes, this herb collection can be divided and replanted once the plants become overgrown. However, these herbs were chosen because they should last for several weeks, even months, before they need division. What's more, most smell and taste as good as they look.

At the heart, tricolor sage (*Salvia officinalis* 'Tricolor') proudly displays its leaves of pink, cream and green.

They work well with the pink blooms of *Origanum laevigatum* 'Herrenhausen', a highly ornamental marjoram relative. A touch of yellow, courtesy of golden marjoram (*O. vulgare* 'Aureum'), peeps above the semi-tumbling form of a variegated culinary thyme (*Thymus × citriodorus* 'Silver Queen'). On the other side, the edible white flowers and slender leaves of Chinese or garlic chives (*Allium tuberosum*) rise above the purple heads of

Viola 'Prince Henry', a flower used for decorating salads and sweet dishes.

Softening the edge of the basket are compact marjoram (*Origanum vulgare* 'Compactum'), a useful culinary form, and white, button-flowered double chamomile (*Chamaemelum nobile* 'Flore Pleno'). Finally, although purely decorative, purple-flowered *Thymus serpyllum* 'Rainbow Falls' forms a trailing cushion of green-and-gold leaves.

While not all herbs are suited to growing in hanging baskets, the vast majority will grow in a container of some kind. Indeed, some more vigorous herbs are best confined to a pot rather than being allowed to run amok in the garden.

Mint (*Mentha*) is difficult to control, yet in a container its vigor can be easily curbed. Marjoram (*Origanum vulgare*, pictured above) and lemon balm (*Melissa officinalis*) are similarly unstoppable. Keep them in their own separate containers.

An herb garden for all your culinary needs can be planted in a collection of containers – it can even be grown in a traditional strawberry planter with side pockets. Matching hanging baskets and troughs will provide additional space. Most herbs demand a sunny position, but a few – including chervil (*Anthriscus cerefolium*), chives (*Allium schoenoprasum*), feverfew (*Tanacetum parthenium*), lemon balm and most mints – will tolerate at least some shade. All appreciate a moisture-retentive soil but resent being waterlogged, so ensure that there is plenty of drainage material in the base of the container.

Tender herbs grown in pots, such as myrtle (*Myrtus communis*) and lemon verbena (*Aloysia triphylla*), can be brought indoors for the winter. Similarly, commonly used evergreens such as bay (*Laurus nobilis*), thyme (*Thymus*) and rosemary (*Rosmarinus officinalis*) can be brought under glass in winter to ensure a fresh supply of leaves.

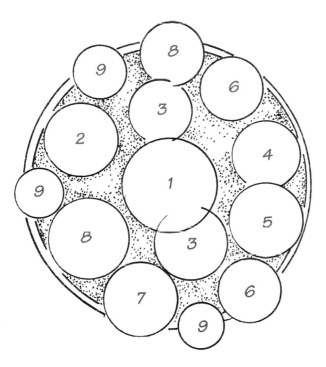

planting key

1 *Salvia officinalis* 'Tricolor'
2 *Origanum vulgare* 'Aureum'
3 *Origanum laevigatum* 'Herrenhausen'
4 *Allium tuberosum*
5 *Viola* 'Prince Henry'

6 *Chamaemelum nobile* 'Flore Pleno'
7 *Origanum vulgare* 'Compactum'
8 Variegated lemon thyme *Thymus × citriodorus* 'Silver Queen'
9 *Thymus serpyllum* 'Rainbow Falls'

Salad basket

Few things are more satisfying than stepping outside your back door and picking fresh ingredients for a meal. No matter how restricted your space may be, this compact basket of salad fare is the perfect way to grow just a few garnishes and salad crops. And they look just as good as they taste.

Parsley (*Petroselinum crispum*) is an exceptionally useful garnish, and its bright green, crinkled leaves are the perfect accompaniment to the small, bright red fruits of trailing tomatoes such as 'Tumbler' or 'Tumbling Tom Red'. There is also a yellow-fruited variety called 'Tumbling Tom Yellow', so if you wish you could fill your basket just with tomatoes to provide a colorful, summer-long supply of sweet fruits.

When it comes to flavor, sweet basil (*Ocimum basilicum*) is in a class of its own, but it does have a reputation for being temperamental and dislikes overwatering and windy sites. For these reasons, plant it in a separate pot and sink it into the soil at the back of the basket, so that you can regulate the watering and replace it easily should it start to suffer. For best results, put the basket in a warm, sheltered spot.

To brighten both your basket and your salads, nasturtiums (*Tropaeolum majus*) and pot or English marigolds (*Calendula*) are ideal. Nasturtium leaves have a peppery taste and, like the calendula, has edible flowers. Both will run riot if you overfertilize them, so an occasional liquid feeding is adequate. Instead, concentrate your efforts on the hungrier tomatoes growing on the opposite side of the basket.

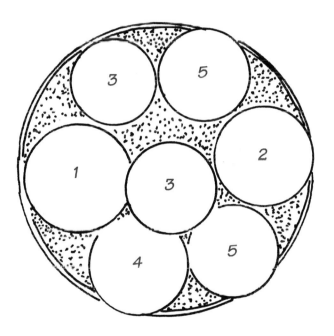

planting key

1 *Calendula* 'Pygmy' mixed
2 *Ocimum basilicum*
3 *Petroselinum crispum*
4 Tomato 'Tumbler'
5 *Tropaeolum* Jewel Series

plant close-up

EDIBLE FLOWERS

When it comes to improving the look of salads, flowers can be as useful as leaves. A surprising number of flowers will not only brighten the bowl but also add a whole new range of flavors.

Perhaps the best-known edible blooms are those of nasturtiums (*Tropaeolum majus*). Along with the buds, they enliven with a mild peppery flavor. Equally effective, the individual petals of pot or calendula (*Calendula* spp.) look great sprinkled among assorted lettuce leaves and dressed with salad oil. They contribute a mild tangy flavor to rice or fish dishes and omelettes. Choose a dwarf, compact type such as *Calendula* 'Pygmy' for containers. Used whole, viola and pansy (*Viola* x *wittrockiana*) flowers make another striking salad addition. Crystallized blooms of the sweet violet (*Viola odorata*) can be used to decorate puddings, cakes and ice creams.

For a mild onion flavor, scatter the pastel-pink petals of chives (*Allium schoenoprasum*, pictured above) over a salad, or use the starry white flowers of Chinese chives (*Allium tuberosum*) to add a hint of garlic. Although too tall for hanging baskets, borage (*Borago officinalis*) and viper's bugloss (*Echium vulgare*) can be grown successfully in other containers and both bear blue flowers that can be added to salads or crystallized for cake decoration. Young borage leaves bring an extra cooling effect and a flavor of cucumber to cold drinks, while their flowers can be floated on the surface for decoration.

Up the garden wall

Hanging baskets are labor intensive, but wall baskets and wall pots can create a similar effect without being quite as demanding. Because they are not subjected to wind and sun from all angles, the soil mix does not dry out quite as quickly. Consequently they are an easy, effective way to liven up a wall.

This trio of wall pots is filled with a mixture of annuals and half-hardy perennials suited to a position in full sun. The largest of the three, a classic, fluted terracotta wall pot, features a dwarf sunflower (*Helianthus annuus* 'Sundance Kid'), which opens its fat buds to reveal flat, round, many-petaled heads of golden yellow and orange-bronze. Running through the center and threading its way up through the sunflowers is *Bidens*

ferulifolia, with yellow, starry flowers on slender stems and filigree foliage.

A tumble of yellow daisy-flowered *Sanvitalia* 'Little Sun' complements the terracotta, while a third trailing plant, *Helichrysum petiolare* 'Limelight', throws long trails of foliage over the side of the pot – a perfect antidote to the otherwise dominant flowers. Except for the sunflowers, where we have used three, each variety is planted singly. Planted in twos or threes, any one of them could be relied upon to fill the pot and look just as pleasing as the mixture shown here.

The second pot, glazed in blue and cream, hosts gentian-blue *Anagallis* 'Skylover' and *Convolvulus sabatius*, a trailer clustered with pale blue saucer-shaped blooms that open wide in the sun. *Koeleria glauca*, a tufty, blue-gray grass, fills the third pot, marrying together the yellows and blues in the other containers.

HELICHRYSUMS

A diverse group of annuals, perennials and sub-shrubs, helichrysums and their relatives range from papery "everlasting" flowers suitable for drying, through trailing kinds ideal for hanging baskets, to sun-loving shrubs such as the silver-leaved curry plant (*H. italicum* subsp. *serotinum*). The main requirement of helichrysums is full sun and good drainage.

H. 'Schwefelicht' (pictured above) is a clump-forming perennial whose white-woolly stems and leaves and pale, sulphur-yellow blooms provide a long season of interest. Renamed *Ozothamnus rosmarinifolius*, *H. rosmarinifolium* is an upright shrub from Australia suitable for larger containers. Its dark green, rosemary-like leaves are joined in early summer by clusters of white, fragrant flowers. *O. r.* 'Silver Jubilee' is a superb variety with silver leaves.

Most useful for containers, especially hanging baskets, are the forms of *H. petiolare*, a mound-forming, frost-tender evergreen. The species bears trailing stems clothed with oval, felty silver-gray leaves. *H. p.* 'Limelight' has lime-yellow leaves and those of *H. p.* 'Variegatum' have creamy margins. *H. p.* 'Roundabout' is a dwarf sport of the latter, growing just 6 inches high and 12 inches across. Although grown for their leaves, small yellow flowers often appear in late summer.

The annual kinds with "everlasting" flowers, suitable for drying (*H. bracteatum*), are now listed under *Xerochrysum bracteatum*, for instance, *X. bracteatum* 'Coca'.

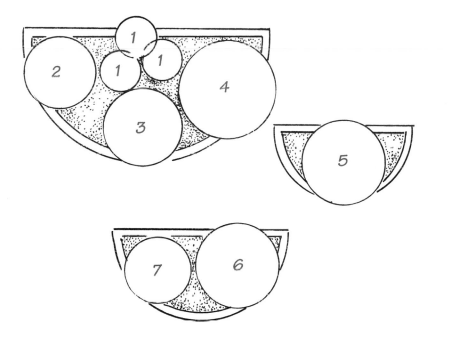

planting key

1 *Helianthus annuus* 'Sundance Kid'
2 *Bidens ferulifolia*
3 *Sanvitalia* 'Little Sun'
4 *Helichrysum petiolare* 'Limelight'
5 *Koeleria glauca*
6 *Anagallis* 'Skylover'
7 *Convolvulus sabatius*

Fabulous foliage

**Not all hanging baskets have to be outdoors –
most greenhouses have room for at least one.
Enclosed porches, with little floor space but the
need for adornment, are also suitable.**

This basket of houseplants is tailored to a greenhouse
where the temperature is maintained at a minimum of
50°F (10°C). Because the plants have been chosen for
their leaves, this basket will look equally good in all
seasons. Open-sided mesh baskets are not ideal indoors;
instead, use a large hanging pot, preferably with a drip-
saucer attached. Choose a light, airy spot and make sure
the hook or bracket that holds the basket is secure.

The stars of this basket are two fancy-leaved begonias.
Begonia 'Merry Christmas' bears large, handsome leaves

8 inches long that are predominantly deep pink but outlined with emerald-green. Dark red centers and leaf margins complete the colorful effect. Pale pink flowers are a bonus in early autumn. The spirally arranged, silver-spotted, dark green leaves of *B.* 'Princess of Hanover' provide an eye-catching contrast.

Less fussy in its needs, the spider plant (*Chlorophytum comosum* 'Vittatum') has a strikingly different form. Its narrow, blade-like, cream-and-light-green leaves erupt here from among the begonias. *Tradescantia zebrina* 'Quadricolor' softens the solid lines of the container. Its trailing stems are clothed in leaves echoing the colors of the begonias.

A second basket, adding more contrast of color and form, holds *Begonia imperialis* with its pale green leaves irregularly splashed with silvery green.

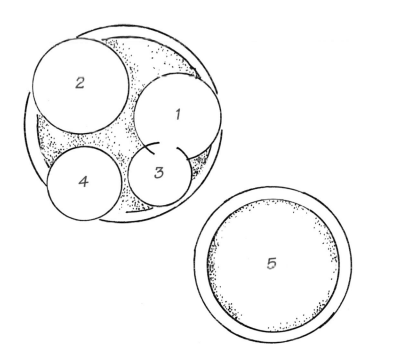

planting key

1 *Begonia* 'Princess of Hanover'
2 *Begonia* 'Merry Christmas'
3 *Chlorophytum comosum* 'Vittatum'
4 *Tradescantia zebrina* 'Quadricolor'
5 *Begonia imperialis*

plant close-up

FANCY-LEAVED BEGONIAS

Begonias, in many of their various guises, are prime candidates for containers and most grow well in hanging baskets. Though renowned for their showy, brightly colored blooms, one of the most impressive groups of begonias is the foliage kind. They display remarkably varied, heart-shaped leaves. Some are spotted, others prominently veined or banded to varying degrees with silver, gold, bronze or pinkish-red. Leaf surfaces range from bright and glossy, almost metallic, to waxy or hairy.

In common with other begonias, fancy-leaved types are easy to grow but fairly short-lived, lasting for an average of 12 months or so. Fortunately, they are easy to propagate either from leaf cuttings or by dividing established plants when repotting. To avoid scorching, place the plants in a bright spot out of direct sunlight and mist the air around them (but not the leaves themselves) regularly to provide humidity. Water sparingly in winter but keep consistently moist from spring to autumn, allowing the surface of the soil to dry out between waterings.

Numerous varieties are available, including *B.* 'Président Carnot' with green and silver leaves; silver, purple and pink *B.* 'Bettina Rothschild' (pictured above); and wine-red, silver-banded *B.* 'Helen Lewis'. *B. masoniana* is known as the 'iron cross begonia' due to the dark brown, cross-like marking that decorates each hairy, deep green, crinkled leaf.

Winter green

In frost-free climates, all of these plants fare well through the darker months, brightening up a wall in winter. As a bonus, all of them can be planted in the garden in spring.

In the short term at least, many dwarf and slow-growing conifers – especially the prostrate kinds – will grow happily in hanging baskets and similar containers. *Juniperus squamata* 'Blue Star', a half-spreading, half-upright mound of blue-gray, is the focus in one wall cone. The contrasting form of *Carex conica* 'Snowline', an evergreen grass with narrow, silver-white margined leaves, arches over the edge and merges with the juniper.

Continuing the silver theme is *Lamium maculatum* 'Beacon Silver', a form of deadnettle with silvered leaves

and pink flowers in spring. Through the sides are *Ajuga reptans* 'Multicolor' and *A. r.* 'Valfredda', their variously colored, crinkled foliage contributing a range of dark and light tones. The former lives up to its name, with foliage randomly decorated in wine-red, cream and green, while the latter has smaller leaves of chocolate-brown. In spring, both bear spikes of blue flowers. Trails of *Vinca minor* 'Alba Variegata' complete the basket.

Even in winter, the bright green foliage of *Santolina rosmarinifolia* subsp. *rosmarinifolia* appears soft and fresh. Here it fills the top of the second basket, offering a foil to the relatively coarse, claret-red-and-silver leaves of *Ajuga reptans* 'Burgundy Glow'. A repeat of *Carex conica* 'Snowline' links the two baskets and *Vinca minor* 'Aureovariegata' echoes the first basket but displays leaves that are variegated bright yellow.

plant close-up

WINTER FOLIAGE

Evergreen foliage plants can liven up any winter display by providing leaf color at a time when flowers are scarce. Grouped together they can create contrasts of tone, texture and form.

All evergreens in containers appreciate a sheltered place during winter, especially in frost-prone or windy locations. Unlike deciduous plants, they still need water in winter, so they may need some watering even in the wettest, coldest months.

Dwarf evergreen shrubs and conifers are among the best plants for foliage appeal and include such stalwarts as hebes and variegated euonymus. Many grasses are also evergreen and their flowing forms are a useful contrast to the more rigid shapes of the shrubs and conifers.

Many shrubby herbs, especially sages (*Salvia*) and thymes (*Thymus*), are reliable provided they do not get too wet. Summer-flowering heathers (*Calluna*) can also be used for their colorful foliage, as can many winter heaths (*Erica*, pictured above). You can also add pieces cut from garden shrubs to the container to improve the display temporarily.

Some low-growing, carpeting perennials are also good as trailing plants for baskets. Among them are bugle (*Ajuga*), deadnettle, periwinkle (*Vinca*), thymes, creeping Jenny (*Lysimachia nummularia*), *Euphorbia myrsinites*, stonecrop (*Sedum*) and variegated London pride (*Saxifraga x urbium* 'Variegata').

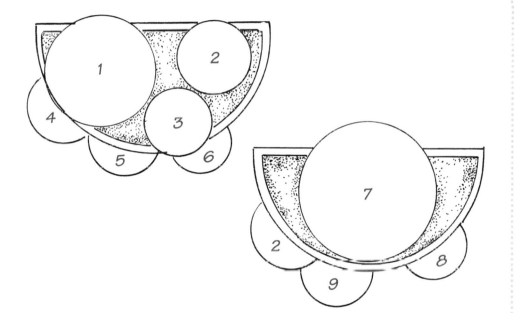

planting key

1 *Juniperus squamata* 'Blue Star'
2 *Carex conica* 'Snowline'
3 *Lamium maculatum* 'Beacon Silver'
4 *Ajuga reptans* 'Multicolor'
5 *Ajuga reptans* 'Valfredda'
6 *Vinca minor* 'Alba Variegata'
7 *Santolina rosmarinifolia* subsp.
   rosmarinifolia

8 *Ajuga reptans* 'Burgundy Glow'
9 *Vinca minor* 'Aureovariegata'

acknowledgments

Mark Bolton 13 top left, 23, 27, 31, 49, 81, 95, 107, 109, 11 top, 14.
Eric Crichton 115.
Garden Picture Library /Brian Carter 105, /John Glover 57, /Neil Holmes 53, 83, /Lamontagne 6, /Howard Rice 47, /Friedrich Strauss 5.
John Glover 77, /Designer: Dan Pearson /RHS Chelsea Flower Show 1993 16 bottom.
Octopus Publishing Group Limited /Mark Bolton /Richmond Adult Community College /RHS Hampton Court Flower Show 2001 1, 13 top right, /Mark Bolton /Topiary By Design /RHS Hampton Court Flower Show 2001 9 top right, 69, 97, /Jerry Harpur 43, 101, /Andrew Lawson 33, /David Sarton /Designer: Natalie Charles /RHS Chelsea Flower Show 2002 3 left, 10 top, /Mark Winwood 16 top, /Steve Wooster 2, 3 right, 9 left, /Mel Yates 12.
Jerry Harpur 45, 75, /Bourton House 99, /Richard Hartlage, Seatle 9 bottom right, /Tom Hobbs, Vancouver 37, /Designer: Anne Alexander-Sinclair 8, 20-21, /Peter Wooster, Connecticut, USA 17
Marcus Harpur 19, 29, 51, 65, 73, 85, 89, 103, 117, 125, /Henry & Ann Bradshaw, Coltishall, Norfolk, UK 61, /Beth Chatto, Essex 91, /Bunny Guinness, RHS Chelsea Flower Show 13 bottom right, /Park Farm 87, /RHS Chelsea Flower Show 1996 70-71, /Designer: Susan Rowley 10 bottom, /Dr. Chris Grey-Wilson 119, /Designer: Stephen Woodhams/ RHS Chelsea Flower Show 2000 7.
Holt Studios International /Willam Harinck 59.
Andrew Lawson 11 bottom, 18, 25, 39, 41, 55, 63, 67, 93, 111, 113, 121.
Derek St Romaine 79.
Harry Smith Collection 35, 123.

Executive Editor: Sarah Ford
Editor: Joss Waterfall
Executive Art Editor: Joanna Bennett
Designer: Ginny Zeal
Production Controller: Viv Cracknell
Picture Researcher: Zoë Holtermann
Color illustrations: Gill Tomblin
Black and white illustrations: Bob Purnell